URBAN EDUCATION: PROBLEMS AND PROSPECTS

URBAN EDUCATION: PROBLEMS AND PROSPECTS

WILLIAM M. PEREL
Wichita State University

PHILIP D. VAIRO
The University of Tennessee at Chattanooga

DAVID McKAY COMPANY, INC.
NEW YORK

URBAN EDUCATION: PROBLEMS AND PROSPECTS

The child was diseased at birth, stricken with a hereditary ill that only the most vital men are able to shake off. I mean poverty—the most deadly and prevalent of all diseases.

EUGENE O'NEILL

Preface

Urban education is difficult to portray because it has so many different manifestations. However, the need to attempt a discussion of the urban phenomenon, while difficult and frustrating, is both challenging and necessary. The undertaking of this volume has special meaning to the authors. They are both products of urban society, and most of their professional associations have been with urban schools and universities. However, the motivating force for this volume is simply the hope of the authors that urban schools and universities will offer educational opportunity to the many who otherwise might never have the chance.

Though much is known and much has been written about urban education, this volume attempts to identify and discuss the basic problems which have to be solved if, in the future, urban education is to fulfill the high hopes of the citizens who reside in the urban complex. It is hoped that this approach will give the reader additional insights and a realistic understanding of the various forces and factors which operate in the urban community.

Many of our citizens believe that the public school is, categorically, the purest symbol of American democracy. The school's role is basic and essential in promoting upward social mobility and equal opportunity among the American people. Today, education, not cheap land, frontiers, rugged individualism, nor expanding business opportunities, plays the important part in providing this mobility and opportunity for all, in the eyes of the American people. Americans are making a sacrifice to provide public schools for their children. Parents want their children to have educational opportunities which they missed themselves. Education, then, has become the most sought after commodity in American life. Looking to the future of America, there is no single feature more important than the school in promoting equal opportunity for all. With this thought in mind, it should be clear that the public school cannot be used for the advancement of one particular group or social class or in an effort to maintain or support the social status quo.

Americans more and more are becoming an urban people. Each federal census shows an increase in population of our metropolitan population centers and a further decline in rural population. Thus, increasingly, education in the United States will be urban education.

The urban school has played a special and strategic role in American life. It has provided some opportunity for upward mobility of the lower class groups. It has been perhaps the most effective democratizing agency in our society. Through several decades it has provided the old immigrants with the necessary skills and knowledge which they needed to function effectively in America, and it has helped them to become assimilated. But the problem today is that the urban school no longer seems able to serve the newer immigrants to our cities. The Negroes, the Puerto Ricans, and all the other underprivileged and socially disadvantaged groups of the inner city are becoming alienated from the urban school; they are alienated from the very agency which most purports to help them. At the same time, the urban school has lost the confidence of the middle class. If the urban school has lost its position of pre-eminence and even of relevance, is it not time that we examine its purposes and goals?

The urban school is called upon to serve a dual role. It must do more than fulfill its traditional role of teaching subject matter to those students able to learn. It is also called upon to assist other students, who have been deprived, handicapped by background, prejudice, or other means, but are able to learn. Certain questions arise. Are these roles incompatible? Why are the underprivileged being alienated from the urban school? How do the new immigrants differ from the old, who found the urban school satisfactory? Is the urban school meeting its responsibilities? Can it meet them? Are those charged with the responsibility of administering the urban schools aware that a problem exists, and are they attempting or proposing solutions? Above all, what is and what should be the role of education in our urban centers for today and for tomorrow?

No institution in American life is called upon to serve so many needs, to fulfill so many aspirations, and to provide such a variety of services. At no time in our history has so heavy a burden of responsibility been placed on one institution as is today placed on the urban school. The very faith which Americans have had in education and in their public school system for so many years makes the burden of responsibility that much heavier.

The eyes of the nation are now on our metropolitan centers of population. These have been and should continue to be educational and cultural centers as well as centers of population and employment. In the years ahead, the urban school must respond to the challenges which it faces, in order to regain its position as the pacesetter for American education. Without the homogenizing influence of the urban schools, our cities cannot remain the melting pots in which persons of different ethnic and social backgrounds mingle. And without such mingling, our cities will become something quite different from what we have known them to be.

It should be evident that this book is the result of the work, devotion, and advice of many of our colleagues and friends. Its preparation was a joint effort to which the authors have contributed equally. Acknowledgment is made to our wives for their continued encouragement and support. We are further indebted to Maurine Gist for her careful typing of the manuscript.

WILLIAM M. PEREL

PHILIP D. VAIRO

February, 1969

Contents

URBAN EDUCATION: PROBLEMS AND PROSPECTS

CHAPTER I

The Flight of the Middle Class

Although many of our citizens, and particularly our politicians, would like to believe that the United States has achieved a classless society, most sociologists who have studied the problem of class in the United States have come to believe that we do have well-defined classes. However, scholars differ as to their number and description.

Most of the literature on the subject seems to describe three classes: the real upper class, the middle class, and the lower class. In recent times, the middle class has been further divided into the upper middle and the lower middle classes. Some authorities believe that the great uncrossable barrier is actually between the two parts of the middle class, this barrier being the college degree. But we propose to consider both parts of the middle class together, while realizing that differences exist.

The aforementioned classes are variously described, but the usual criteria include occupation, education, source of income, and type of residence. Surprisingly enough, amount of income is often not mentioned, except as it may influence type of residence and be influenced by the remaining criteria. Equally surprising, religious, racial, and ethnic backgrounds are not mentioned.

As we shall use the term "middle class," we shall mean primarily persons whose income may be described as being in the "middle range" of incomes. This range cannot be defined precisely, partly because it can vary greatly from one section of the country to another. However, we are talking about people who are moderately well off, without being in any sense rich.

While much has been written of the beliefs which such persons are supposed to hold and of the ethnic, cultural, and political backgrounds of such persons, the middle income group contains almost the entire spectrum in each of these other areas. Any attempt to identify the middle class individual with the WASP (White-Anglo-Saxon-Protestant) individual is likely to introduce troublesome counterexamples. Certainly the Negro, the Jew, the Latin American, and the Chinese or Japanese encounters special problems of status, and such an individual is not always easily accorded the status to which his income would entitle him, were he a WASP. Also, racial, ethnic, and religious minorities tend to be overrepresented in the lower class and underrepresented numerically in the middle class. But the middle class does contain persons of all races, all religions, and all national origins.

In recent years the so-called "middle class values" have been under attack. One hears disparaging comments about middle class values and middle class prejudices in theatrical and literary circles. Plays and novels have been written to describe the status striving, the meaningless political, social, and even sexual activities of middle class individuals, with their automobiles, their barbecue grills, and their keeping up with the Joneses. Disparaging comments are frequently made about middle class people, and they are often called defamatory names, particularly in the writings of the far left and the so-called "New Left." The membership of the New Left consists primarily of the children of middle class parents, so it might be assumed that they, at least, know what they are talking about. And finally, it has been the middle class, and not the upper class, which has been the chief enemy of Communism in all its forms and which has been recognized as such by Communists, beginning with Karl Marx.

Yet the emergence of the middle class, beginning in the Renaissance, is usually given as one of the causes of the development of the democratic political institutions which are now fairly common in the Western world. And it is the absence of a large middle class which is usually given as the explanation for the feudalism of nineteenth-century Russia and for the appeal of Communism in many underdeveloped countries. The importance of middle class individuals in the development of our own political system and the credit given to such persons by writers of our own revolutionary period, including especially Thomas Jefferson, is already well known.

Thomas Jefferson had been to France and seen the great masses of people in Paris, the proletariat, without property and without hope or stake in the society of which they were a part. While he wrote and spoke of the possible necessity of further revolutions in this country, he nevertheless believed that our large middle class and upward mobility would prevent the excesses of the French Revolutionary period.

To an extent, the authors believe that the so-called middle class values are actually the ideologies and values of mainstream America. It is not claimed that all such values are good or desirable. But those who would enter the middle class, as it is currently constituted, must understand and come to terms with them, even if they do not actually accept them. The foreign immigrants who have been assimilated have often adopted such values very quickly in order to enter the mainstream of American life. Once during a Texas election, an immigrant, who had been in this country less than ten years, was asked why he would not vote for the Mexican-American, Henry B. Gonzalez, who was a candidate for governor. He replied, "Don't you remember the Alamo?" Many of the members of other minority groups have not been able to adapt themselves to our mores so quickly.

The middle class individual may be of any racial, ethnic, or national origin. He may be newly arrived in the middle class or may be descended from many generations of middle class ancestors. It is important to realize that sometimes persons newly arrived in this group are more militantly middle class than those who have long been accustomed to membership in this group. Those in the lower middle class by reason of the lack of a college degree may reasonably expect their children to obtain degrees and so become upper middle class.

The authors have found, in their experience at urban universities, a great number of students whose parents never went to college. In one such university, the New Orleans campus of Louisiana State University, the overwhelming majority of the students were the children of noncollege-educated parents. Fordham University, which traditionally has educated the children of immigrant parents, is now moving to assist the Negro and Puerto Rican segment of New York City's population. Many such students have graduated and moved into the upper middle class. Thus, the great barrier between lower and upper middle class groups may be bridged in a second generation. Middle class people, whether college-educated or not, are interested in education, including higher education for their children. Furthermore, they are likely to be knowledgeable in educational matters.

The middle class group furnishes our society with a large number of its professionals. Most of our physicians, lawyers, engineers, teachers at all levels, from elementary school to graduate school, and by far the greatest number of our white-collar and more highly skilled blue-collar workers come from this group. The middle class individual is likely to be active and interested in civic, cultural, and, to a limited extent, philanthropic activities in his community. He is likely to be a homeowner or to aspire to homeownership. As a homeowner, he is concerned vitally in such matters as police and fire protection. At least in a smaller community, he is likely to serve on the school board or the library board, where his interest and education can make a contribution to the life of the community.

The middle class individual differs markedly from the upper class or truly rich individual. Many sociologists have pointed out their differences in vocabulary and manner of speech, in types of recreation, in politics, in reading habits, and so on. The rich man is likely to have more than one home and find his interests divided among several cities. He may be in the very highest management circles of one of our largest corporations. He will almost certainly live either in an exclusive apartment building in the city or on an estate at its edge, if indeed he does not maintain both. Thus, in New York City, the really rich people who live in Manhattan look down from their apartments on Central Park, where it is not safe to walk at night.

The rich man does not usually send his children to the public schools and is, therefore, unlikely to take much interest in them. Although many rich persons are civic-minded and may also make themselves available to serve on committees, commissions, and school boards, they are, in essence, really removed from the "nuts and bolts" issues facing the people, and especially the middle class people of the city. The rich or the upper middle class individual may be the mayor of a city or serve on its school board, and yet send his children to a private school. The rich, unlike the middle class, usually have access to those charged with the responsibility of running the city, whenever the need arises, without any continuing effort on their part. In fact, the rich may be closely associated with the power structure of the city, if not actually identical with it.

At the other end of the spectrum one finds the extremely poor. Again, there are many exceptions, but among the poor are found those who either are unemployed or work in the most menial jobs. Here are the people without influence, without education, and without any apparent stake in the community. Within the city, the poor are unlikely to own their homes. Normally they live in tenements or in shoddy houses, often known as "rent houses," because it is clear that no one who could afford to own a house would live in one of them. Because such persons have no money, no power, and no influence, they are likely to be denied their fair share of the city services. Thus, the police protection, the fire protection, and the sanitation services provided by the city are usually less available to the poor. Their garbage is not picked up as regularly. Their streets are not cleaned as carefully or as often. The snow is not removed from their streets and sidewalks as it is in other parts of the city. Such persons not only are unlikely to be members of the school board but are unlikely to have influence with the school board or with any other city agency. Their children go to public schools, if they go at all.

Some changes in this pattern are taking place. In 1968, Mayor John Lindsay appointed a Negro postman, who sends his children to public schools, to the New York City Board of Education. But the unusual nature of such an appointment is clearly shown by the publicity given to this appointment and to the occupation and race of the appointee. Negro, Puerto Rican, Mexican-American, and even WASP members of the working class are not often appointed to city school boards, even though their children constitute an ever growing majority of the urban school population.

The public schools, which the children of the poor attend, are likely to be housed in old buildings, if only because the poor live in the older sections of the city. Such buildings are often not kept in the best repair and may lack some of the niceties of the schools which serve middle class children. If the children of the poor happen to be integrated in the same school with middle class or upper class children, they are the children who are called reluctant learners, underachievers, nonacademic-minded, slow, disadvantaged, culturally deprived, laggers, and sometimes just "dumb." These are the children who are apt to present behavioral problems to the middle class teachers. Their truancy is high, and their participation in the social life of the school is likely to be low.

The parents in poor neighborhoods may desire good education for their children, but, lacking education themselves, they may not always be able to determine whether or not their children are getting a good education. Even if they were, they would be unlikely to gain a hearing before anyone of sufficient power, influence, and sympathy to achieve any desirable change.

Sometimes their difficulty in approaching persons in authority is compounded by their ethnic or racial backgrounds and even by their inability to speak proper English. This latter problem is very severe in Spanish Harlem and in some of the larger cities of the Southwest, particularly in Texas, where vast numbers of Spanish-speaking citizens reside. However, it is interesting to note that as minority groups in our urban centers begin to organize, as have Negro groups under the Black Power slogan, they have increasingly been able to gain an audience with elected officials and even to elect one of their own number to a position of authority. School boards are early targets of the political arm of such groups.

The poor often lack money for automobiles, and other forms of transportation are becoming less and less available in many cities or more and more expensive. Thus, the poor individual finds it difficult to leave his neighborhood. He must, therefore, buy most of his groceries, clothing, furniture, and other merchandise from neighborhood stores and must pay whatever he is charged. Lacking ready money, he must rely on credit and must pay whatever credit charges are demanded of him. Offices of small loan companies and pawnshops are likely to be common in such neighborhoods, for obvious reasons. Of course, what effect the new federal Truth in Lending Act, recently passed by Congress, will have on credit and interest charges is not now possible to determine.

One of the strengths of American society has always been the possibility of upward mobility, even though the Horatio Alger stories might never have been true. It cannot be expected that every citizen can rise from poor to rich, from lower class to upper class. However, it would certainly seem to be both possible and desirable to accelerate the upward mobility from the lower economic classes to middle class status. Such upward mobility has always been possible in the United States and probably to a greater extent than in any other country in the history of the world. Even when our country consisted of thirteen English colonies, it was possible for the new arrival to move from indentured servant to landowner within a single generation. It is pretended that such upward mobility is still universally possible. However, it is surely obvious that some groups have had considerably more difficulty than have others.

Until World War II, the middle class element tended to dominate the public image of our largest cities. The rich man was elected to political office only if he made some attempt to appease and satisfy the middle class. When the poor man was elected to public office, as sometimes happened, he immediately became middle class, just as he became middle class if he entered one of the professions. But, it should be pointed out that a poor man is increasingly unlikely to become an elected official or even a serious candidate.

Successful campaigns require television coverage, campaign workers, and a source of income for the candidate to enable him to support his family while he is engaging in full-time campaigning. Vast sums of money are needed and are usually spent even in local campaigns, to say nothing of state contests. The poor are not even represented at national nominating conventions, as the cost of being a delegate is prohibitive for them.

If the successful politician either is or becomes middle class, it would seem that an enormous increase in the percentage of citizens of a city holding middle class status would increase the level of democracy practiced within the city. However, beginning in the mid-1930's and accelerating even more rapidly since, the middle class element in the central city has been declining. This phenomenon can be observed in every one of our largest cities, particularly in the northern part of the United States. Although this phenomenon began in the 1930's, it was not immediately noticed, and the greatest comment on this subject occurred after the results of the 1960 census were known.

What is happening is that the middle class is leaving the city and fleeing to the suburbs in ever increasing numbers. Thus, in the 1960 census, twelve of the twenty largest cities in the United States showed a decrease in population from 1950 to 1960, in spite of the fact that the nation as a whole experienced an enormous growth in population. The metropolitan areas of these cities did not decrease in population, but gained. However, the shift in population was from the city itself to its suburbs. Some of the losses in population were substantial. Every single one of our twenty largest cities outside of the deep South, excepting only Los Angeles, showed a net loss in population from 1950 to 1960. What population shifts have taken place during the 1960's cannot be definitely known until after the 1970 census, but there is every indication that a further decline in the population of our major cities has taken place.

This trend in population shift was well established, even during the 1940's, although many believed that this phenomenon in the forties was simply a wartime aberration. In any case, from 1940 to 1950, the United States as a whole showed a 14.5 percent increase in population and the central cities a 13.8 percent increase, while the so-called "rings" around cities showed a 34.2 percent increase. But now, instead of increasing at a lower rate, the central city is actually declining in population, so the trend in population shift is even more clear.

The middle class is highly mobile. In some middle class neighborhoods, it has been found that 80 percent of the families have lived in their homes for less than five years, compared with only 25 percent in working class neighborhoods. The middle class is rootless—more so that ever before in our history. Many companies move their junior executives from place to place as part of their training programs. A former colleague of one of the authors, who left academia to work for International Business Machines, Incorporated, once remarked after a year or so with the company that I.B.M. stood for "I'll be moving." But for whatever reason, the middle class individual is no longer tied to a single section of the nation, and it is not surprising that he no longer feels the old loyalty to the city or neighborhood of his birth.

Forty years ago, the home buyer expected to live in his home until he retired or died. Today, the building industry seeks in its advertising to persuade the homeowner to "trade up." Some of the techniques of home salesmanship have been borrowed from the automobile salesroom. Today, the home buyer expects to buy a nicer house in a more prestigious neighborhood as his status rises, or perhaps a larger house as his family grows, or a smaller house as his family shrinks again. The new developments in the suburbs are where one must look for the greatest choice in neighborhoods and housing types.

The figures given above refer to population shifts; but how can it be known that it is the middle class that has moved? There is every reason to believe that the loss in middle class population has been even greater than the census figures indicate for the net population. For the most part, the departing middle class citizens have been replaced, if at all, by poor southern Negroes, Puerto Ricans, and Mexican-Americans coming to the cities with the hope of greater employment opportunities and/or unemployment and welfare benefits. Although not easy to document, there is even a tendency for middle class persons to move from the core of the city to its outskirts, even when they do not remove themselves into the suburbs.

An examination of federal census data clearly shows that the people who live in suburbs are statistically very different from those who live in the city. The following data are based on a study of every metropolitan area in the United States with a population of 500,000 or more by the 1960 census. Suburban cities were included in the study if their population was 40,000 or more.

In both the 1950 and 1960 census, it appears that the resident of the suburb is more likely to be married than the resident of the city and less likely to be single, widowed, or divorced. In 1950, 99.2 percent of the suburban population was white, compared with 90.6 percent for the metropolitan area as a whole. The corresponding figures for 1960 are 98.8 percent and 87.42 percent. While it appears that from 1950 to 1960 there has been some increase in the suburban nonwhite population, the fact is that the suburban increase has not kept pace with the increase in the metropolitan area.

Since we are associating middle class status primarily with income and to a lesser extent with occupation, we may examine these factors in the suburbs and in the metropolitan areas. Thus in 1950 the percentage of wage earners in both groups earning in excess of $10,000 was virtually identical: 4.36 percent in the suburbs and 4.14 percent in the metropolitan area; but by 1960 the corresponding figures were 22.48 percent and 20.48 percent.

Another indication of the change is the fact that the medians were virtually identical in 1950, $3,007 and $3,006; whereas in 1960 the median income was $7,120 in the suburbs, but only $6,740 in the whole metropolitan area. At the other end of the scale, only 2.17 percent in the suburbs earned less than $1,000, against 3.22 percent in the metropolitan area. In 1950, 44 percent of the wage earners were white collar workers in the suburbs, as against 33.5 percent white collar workers in the metropolitan area. By 1960, the corresponding figures were 49 percent and 39 percent. The most striking difference is in the professional and technical classification, which makes up 17 percent of the suburbs in 1960, but only 11 percent of the metropolitan area population.

The difference is also apparent in education, although here the gap between suburbs and metropolitan area narrowed from 1950 to 1960. But even in 1960, the suburban dweller averaged a year more of formal education and was 50 percent more likely to be a college graduate. Possibly the greater number of young children in the suburbs explains why the differences in education are not even larger.

The suburban dweller is 50 percent more likely to live in a one-family dwelling than is the resident of the metropolitan area, and he is 25 percent more likely to own his home. Although the number of those dwelling in single-family housing has increased from 1950 to 1960 in both the suburbs and the city, the ratio has remained unchanged. Finally, the rent paid by the renter is higher in the suburbs. In 1950 the suburban renter was seven times as likely to pay $100 per month or more in rent as was the average resident of the metropolitan area. This differential decreased considerably by 1960, but was still substantial.

One final difference is in age. The median age difference in 1950 was only three years, but this had increased to ten years by 1960. The biggest difference is found in the age group 0 to 9, which comprised 28 percent of the suburban population, but only 22 percent of the metropolitan area population in 1960. In summary, the suburban dweller is likely to be married and have children, to own his own single-family home, to be a white collar worker, to be better educated than the city dweller; and he is almost certain to be white.

The middle class citizen has the means to escape the city, with its many problems, especially its crimes of violence against both persons and property. One reads of the decay of the core of the city, but whether this decay has caused the exodus of the middle class or been caused by it seems now to be moot and irrelevant.

There are many factors involved, and most of these have been at work for some thirty years. In the first place, the middle class citizen today owns an automobile and often two automobiles, so that he can drive a considerable distance to work, while leaving transportation available to his family. Cities and states, with federal assistance, have built increasingly efficient freeways and interstate highways to make long-distance commuting possible and relatively easy and convenient. Thirty years ago most Americans lived relatively near their work; but today it is not unusual to find persons driving twenty, thirty, forty, or even fifty miles every day to their places of employment.

The very growth of our population centers has itself contributed to the exodus of the middle class. The American ideal has always been to own that little patch of ground, and no class of people adheres so firmly to such ideals as does the middle class. The developers take advantage of this ideal by calling their developments "Sherwood Forest," "Sunny Acres," "Hidden Valley," and even "Pony Ranch." The builders and developers have made moves to the suburbs very attractive to middle class families. Today, the young middle class couple wants a new house filled with the finest appliances already built in. Until very recent times, mortgage money was plentiful, and FHA and GI loans made it possible for even lower middle class families to buy homes which would have been far beyond their means in former years. In particular, provisions of the laws establishing FHA and GI loans favored the purchase of new houses. New houses were to be found only in newly developed areas. The advertising pressure in books and magazines and on television has been enormous. Not only in the advertisements but even in the television soap operas one finds the family, presented as typically American, living in a house which could be found only in a suburb, and one finds the family breadwinner commuting to work.

Another factor is the dirt and smog of the inner city. Only within the past few years or so has any real attention been given to the problem of the pollution of air and water in the large cities. For example, thirty years ago the Lake Michigan beaches in Chicago provided the citizens of Chicago with a splendid recreational facility, right in the heart of the city. But today, the waters of the Lake Michigan are so polluted in the Chicago area that no one would swim there, unless he lacked the means to go elsewhere.

Thirty years ago its was not uncommon to find more than one family living in the same house, even in middle class neighborhoods, and several generations of one family could be found in the same household fairly often. Today, such phenomena are likely only among the poor. Thus, today more housing units are required to house the same number of people. Movement out of the city has been one of the results.

The exodus of the middle class seems to grow of itself. Middle class people tend to associate with other middle class people. When middle class people leave the city, middle class neighborhoods tend to disappear. Middle class people, newly arrived in the city, may not be able to find the middle class neighborhood they seek without buying a home in one of the suburbs. Thus, the suburb has much to offer the middle class citizen, as compared with the city. The suburb gives him a chance to escape the crowded city with its crime, smoke, and pollution, not to mention the riots and other forms of racial unrest. The restrictions in the suburban area seem to promise him stability in the value of his home.

The developer promises the middle class citizen a community in which the other residents will be very like himself in age, interests, and social status. Thus, he can expect that his children will have other children of the same ages with which to play. He can expect to entertain in exactly the same style and manner as his neighbors. Everywhere he looks he will see only an image of himself.

At one time the individualistic American would have viewed being surrounded by other images of himself with some degree of alarm. But contemporary society seems to demand conformity, and most members of the middle class have shown themselves willing to conform in almost all areas of life. The developer may even have provided playgrounds, a swimming pool, tennis courts, and a community clubhouse. His advertising is likely to show an attractive young woman removing groceries from a station wagon (which may even be called a "suburban" or "ranch wagon") in the driveway of one of his houses, and she is sure to be labeled "an attractive suburbanite."

A suburban community must also have its schools. Due to the mass-production techniques of builders, some small villages have been transformed into suburbs very quickly, sometimes increasing in population by a factor of five, or even ten, in only five years. In such cases, particularly where industry is lacking, it has been very difficult to establish a large enough tax base to build and maintain an adequate school system. Older residents of the village, whose children have grown, deeply resent paying the increasing school taxes made necessary by the enormous numbers of children the new residents bring with them. But the builders have helped with the establishment of schools in some developments, and the state government has been willing to make substantial grants to some such local school systems. Thus, the suburban schools do have their problems, as was pointed out by James B. Conant in his book *Slums and Suburbs*; but they do not have the multitude of problems which face the urban schools.

For the most part, suburban schools are good in the general sense of the word. They are good, not because the buildings and equipment are better, but because the children of middle class parents are likely to be better prepared to cope with the requirements of school life, which is essentially middle class in character. Suburban schools are likely to attract more experienced and better-qualified teachers, and teacher turnover is not so great as in the central city. Teachers' salaries in suburbs are competitive with if not higher than those in urban school systems.

The suburban community can almost approximate the Jeffersonian democratic ideal. In such a community, there are few rich and few poor. Usually, there are no slums. The crime rate is considerably lower than in the city, especially as regards crimes of violence. And there is less smoke and dirt, as there is little or no industry. The community can be very much what the citizens want to make of it.

It should be pointed out here that persons who move to such a suburban community in order to totally escape racial integration have usually not been successful in the suburbs of most northern cities. In fact, most such cities take the presence of a Negro lawyer, engineer, or physician as a point of pride. But such integration as exists is not truly significant, because, first, the Negro resident of such a community not only is certain to be middle class or above but is likely to be white in every sense of the word, excepting only the color of his skin; and second, the integration is only token and has very little impact on the community.

But the suburbs do bring about segregation. The middle class not only is segregated from other classes but is itself segregated into subclasses in some metropolitan areas. Sometimes this segregation is racial, ethnic, or even religious in character, and sometimes it represents an occupational or finer economic differentiation. Almost every large metropolitan area has its Jewish suburbs, for example.

Much of such segregation would appear to be by individual choice, but it is nonetheless regrettable. Some such segregation is intended by the developer and is not only not hidden but blatantly advertised. We see developments pictured as containing homes for the "rising young executive" and developments advertised as containing "executive type" homes. If a builder has more than one development, as is not uncommon, his salesman will steer the prospective home buyer to the right development. He may say to the Jew, "You would not be comfortable here, but in this other area you would be very close to the Jewish Community Center."

Some corporations require that their employees live in a suburb appropriate to their level within the company, so that they will have friends neither too high nor too low in the corporation structure. A promotion, then, means a move to a more exclusive suburb, and a new set of friends, and a new set of rules to which conformity is demanded—or so we are told by William H. Whyte, Jr., in his *Organization Man*.

One of the many problems of our age is the integration of our many minorities into a common citizenship. Yet we have divisions of many kinds in our society. The division into economic classes, primarily by means of family income, is usually called "vertical stratification" and has already been discussed. But we also have division into Jew, Negro, Italian-American, Irish-American, Polish-American, and so on, which is sometimes called "horizontal stratification." One of the goals of the socialist is to reduce or minimize vertical stratification. Perhaps the United States, having more ethnic, racial, and religious minorities, has more horizontal stratification than most European countries; but all countries have vertical stratification, even those countries which claim to be socialist. Short of dictatorship, there seems no way to bring about absolute economic equality, and no one is seriously proposing that an attempt in this direction be made. However, it may be hoped that the gaps between vertical classes can be narrowed and that communication between classes can become more meaningful.

On the other hand, the elimination of barriers between and among the various horizontal groupings in our society has been one of the major goals of our national leadership for decades. While considerable progress has been made, much remains undone.

The movement to the suburbs has done a great deal to solidify racial and other segregation. The pattern can be seen most clearly in some of the larger southern cities. The older sections of New Orleans, particularly the French Quarter or Vieux Carré, are as racially integrated as anyone could wish. So are the older sections of Atlanta; but the suburbs of both cities have been totally segregated until very recently. It has only recently been realized that the maintenance of barriers in the horizontal structure tends to contribute to the maintenance of barriers in the vertical structure.

If mingling, friendship, co-operation, and association are to take place between Jew and Gentile, or between white and Negro, it most likely will be between Jew and Gentile or between white and Negro of the same vertical class. The white member of the middle class does not count the man who collects his garbage among his friends, whether he be white or black, Jew or Gentile. Racial and religious integration will be a fact when white and Negro teachers, Jewish and Gentile physicians, can establish contact.

Many of the peculiar notions which the white middle class holds about the Negro actually apply, if at all, to the lowest class Negro, with whom he is more likely to come in contact. It is one of our greatest ironies that our white physician is likely to know more Negro janitors than Negro physicians. He cannot be sure when he attempts to generalize about Negroes that he is not generalizing about janitors. It is known that there were as few Negro physicians and lawyers rioting in Watts as there were white physicians and lawyers. In the Detroit riots during the summer of 1967, not only was the black middle class not in evidence but the white lower class was very much in evidence.

As our suburban or bedroom communities are so often organized today, then, the white Protestant or Catholic middle class individual is segregated not only from other economic classes but even from the Jewish or Negro middle class. Thus, the middle class flight to the suburbs compounds one of our most serious national problems.

Much has been written of the "evils" which are supposedly inherent in suburban life. We are told that our suburbanites do

not lead a worth-while existence and, having left the real problems and the real arena, they now concern themselves with trivia.
They make gardens, whether or not they like gardening. They
all buy barbecue outfits and cook hamburgers in their back
yards. They all buy color television and hi-fi sets and enjoy a
"canned" culture, since they have left the real culture behind in
the city. The female suburbanite wears shorts or slacks and goes
to the supermarket with her hair in curlers. Their homes sit on
little lots in neat rows, each one like every other one except for
superficial differences. Faced with increasingly scarce land near
our larger cities, some of our most noted architects and designers,
especially Frank Lloyd Wright, have proposed all sorts of
complexes to break the individual lot pattern of suburbs and have
told our citizens what they ought to want. The Levittown development on Long Island is "pointed to with pride" or held up as a
"horrible example," depending on one's point of view. But suburban living must also be examined from the point of view of the
suburbanite.

Suburbs are not really new, having been in existence for a
hundred years or more. There were even developers as long ago
as the thirties, although then they usually confined their activities to dividing up property into lots and putting in streets.
It was a long process, however, for the average citizen to save
enough money to buy one of these lots and then arrange for his
own home to be built. So suburbs did not grow very rapidly and
did not attract the middle class until developers began to build
houses on their property and until FHA mortgages became
available.

Immediately after World War II, the returning veterans began
to establish families and to demand housing. With the GI Bill
of Rights to assist them, many of these new families demanded
the right to purchase homes. When Levittown was started, these
veterans stood in line to buy their own homes for $6,900 and up.
To those used to better houses, Levittown was not very appeal-
ing. But to the New Yorker accustomed to the cramped quarters
of a small Manhattan apartment, the houses seemed so attractive
that the original demand not only continued but increased. The
new homeowners have added on to their homes or otherwise

improved them to the point that they no longer look more alike than do the houses in most other neighborhoods.

In the suburbs, the prices of homes have shown a steady upward trend, so that the new homemaker often finds that he has made an excellent investment. Whether we like it or not, it must be admitted that the city dweller who has moved to a suburb has been, for the most part, satisfied with his move. Were this not the case, the movement to the suburbs would have halted rather than accelerated.

But what has the middle class citizen left behind in the city? Originally, he left behind whatever mystique surrounds the core of the downtown area, with its tall buildings, department stores, theaters, museums, libraries, and other cultural resources. However, today many of the resources of the downtown area have been brought to the suburbs.

The largest department stores have established branches in shopping centers convenient to suburban communities. Some of these stores are truly impressive. Sometimes they are fully as large and much nicer, as they are much newer, than the downtown stores. And anything which is not available in the suburban store can easily be ordered from a downtown store and delivered to the customer's home. Most big city department stores offer free delivery up to a distance of fifty or more miles from the inner city. The absence or the high cost of downtown parking makes downtown shopping much less attractive than it once was. And the suburbanite who commutes to work every day does not find it impossibly difficult to come into the city to attend the theater or to go to a museum or a baseball game once or twice a month.

Not only stores have followed the middle class to the suburbs; so also have employment opportunities. The existence of so many retail establishments in the new suburbs gives employment to many suburbanites. And the offices, laboratories, and research centers of some industries have joined the movement to the suburbs. Many light industries now locate in the suburbs due to the relative cheapness of land, and in recent years new capital industrial investment in the suburbs has exceeded slightly in dollars such investment in the inner city. Finally, the large suburban population naturally attracts professionals of all sorts in sufficient numbers to render the necessary professional services. A consequence of all this is a loss of jobs and payrolls to the city itself.

This movement of the middle class from the city to the suburbs seems so firmly established and has been going on for so long and for so many reasons that we see little likelihood of its being reversed. We expect the exodus of the middle class from the city to continue. Although most civic leaders are now aware of the problem and are making attempts to alleviate some of the causes of the exodus, their efforts have so far been much too little and much too late to have any noticeable effect in the immediate future.

We expect, then, to see the cities become home for only the very poor, the very rich, and perhaps a relatively few unmarried young persons who like the excitement of the city and have less need for the advantages of the suburbs than has the middle class family. The very rich will continue to send their children to private schools, and their children will continue to make use of privately owned recreational facilities for the most part. Thus, more and more, the large city school system will serve only the children of the poor. And the fire protection and police protection and other city services will serve the businesses of the city and the poor people.

The departure of the middle class and the consequent reduction of the value of private homes in the core of the city, together with a loss of taxable property due to the construction of freeways enabling the suburbanite to reach the city, has already led to a lower tax base for the city. The attempts on the part of cities to impose taxes, particularly income taxes, which persons who do not live in the city must pay is a clear indication of this effect.

The absence of a middle class element in the city will be a severe blow to the city's cultural life. There will be fewer and fewer middle class persons available to participate in all the various aspects of city life. Most important, middle class children will not be enrolled in the city schools. Every child who leaves a city school for suburbia takes his parents with him, thus depriving the schools of the traditional support for educational improvement. It will, indeed, become increasingly difficult to achieve the goal of quality, integrated education if the middle class families abandon the city.

It is interesting to note that in the city of Detroit, 20 percent of the teachers in low income neighborhoods (median family income below $7,000) were substitute teachers, whereas only 5.5 percent of the teaching force in the schools of upper income neighborhoods were substitutes.[1] The data collected by Havighurst further support the thesis that the poor receive inadequate education and are taught by less well qualified teachers. In Chicago, the percentage of regular teachers in high income areas is far above the percentage for inner city schools, the range being from 94 down to 64 percent.[2]

The picture is not completely dark. The fact that Gary, Indiana, and Cleveland, Ohio, recently elected Negro mayors indicates that the white middle class will increasingly make possible the election of city officials who more truly represent the poor people of the city. The white middle class is probably motivated in part by the hope that the election of such officials will bring a speedy end to the summer riots. If riots end in Gary and Cleveland, we shall see more of the poor and particularly the Negro leaders elected to high office. But if riots continue anyway, this trend may be reversed. Hopefully, the poor of the cities will be willing to give their own representatives a chance to represent them and to remove many of the obstacles which stand between the poor and upward mobility.

The absence of the bulk of the middle class children in the city schools, elsewhere described as having a debilitating effect on the schools, may make it possible for the schools to provide the special programs and educational opportunities so desperately needed by the culturally deprived and handicapped children of the poor. But it must be remembered that when schools focus on compensatory education, the middle class parents whose children remain in the schools will feel that the curriculum is ignoring the needs of their children, will protest, and may eventually move to the suburbs.

The fact that there is some benefit to the city schools in having a more nearly homogeneous student body should not blind us to the fact that the departure of the middle class from the cities in great numbers is a disaster. The departing middle class leaves behind in the city only the very rich and the very poor, so that city society is becoming almost an exact approximation to the society of eighteenth- and nineteenth-century France, which produced revolution after revolution. When the population of a large city consists almost entirely of the poor who own no property and have no influence and have no stake in society, we have the proletariat of which Karl Marx wrote.

Thomas Jefferson, who had seen the teeming masses of Paris, feared urbanization even in his time because of the possibility of the formation of just such a mass of people as is increasingly coming to populate our larger cities. Abraham Lincoln wrote that a man who does not own a house should not seek to destroy his neighbor's house, but rather should help him to protect it, so that when he acquired a house, it would be secure. However, the great majority of the slum dwellers in our cities not only own no property but have no hope of ever owning property. Middle class values are closely bound up with the ownership of property. Where middle class values dominate a city, the police department strongly protects property and property rights. Those who own no property, have never owned property, and have no real hope of ever owning property, however, cannot be expected to respect property as a sacred value.

The very destructiveness of the poor seems almost contrary to their own self-interest, but it becomes understandable when viewed in the light of the apparent hopelessness of their situation. In the riots in our large cities, particularly during the summer of 1967, the rioters destroyed their own homes and the stores in which they did business. But they regard property as something which belongs to someone else, usually a hated absentee landlord or a store owner who has not always dealt fairly with them. Surrounded by luxury on every side and seeing on television the very same homes and appliances which have helped to attract the middle class to suburbia, the ghetto dweller can only lash out in fury at those who seem to possess that which he does not have and has no hope of getting. If the present trend is allowed to continue indefinitely, our cities are likely to become "off limits" to middle class citizens.

Realizing the problems of a city without a middle class, the leaders of the poor themselves would like to encourage middle class people to remain or to return to the city. While some efforts have been made, it is too soon to see any positive results. Unfortunately, the middle class citizen is likely to be very much interested in law and order and the preservation of private property, particularly after the recent riots. Law and order is not something which sounds very positive to the slum dweller, since to him law and order is likely to represent a policeman who has not always been sympathetic to his problems and may have tended in the past to exhibit a considerable degree of prejudice toward the racial or ethnic group represented by the slum dweller. However, some steps have been taken in an effort to make the city more attractive to the middle class citizen.

But the problem of satisfying the often opposing demands of the middle class and the poor can be very difficult. Mayor Lindsay of New York has been concerned with the problems of the New York poor and has maintained his popularity with the New York slum dweller. Partly because of his concern, New York has managed to avoid the riots which have plagued so many other cities. But the New York middle class has not been pleased by all of his efforts.

In late October, 1968, a meeting of civic leaders in the Borough of Queens was held. In the New York *Times* of November 2, 1968, this meeting was described as a "Middle Class Revolt." This group opposed many of Lindsay's programs designed to assist the poor. It called for an end to attempts at school decentralization, an end to rent control, a reduction of the power of the city's Human Rights Commission, an end to compensatory admission of unqualified Negro and other students to the City University, and an end to "interference of city civilian employees in the operation of the Police Department."

Most of these middle class citizens are sympathetic with the problems of the poor and with the mayor's attempts to aid them. However, they feel he has neglected their needs in order to aid others. The fact that Mr. Lindsay is wealthy has not escaped this group, which claims that he is "too interested in the stylish rich and the striving poor." The needs of the urban middle class cannot be totally ignored, as this group may well elect persons to public office who will serve them even at the expense of ignoring the poor. Certainly, Mayor Lindsay cannot hope for re-election without some middle class support.

Just prior to the 1968 general election, a description of the "average American voter" was published widely in the press, from data obtained from the federal census. Most political figures are well aware that the average voter differs from the average citizen, but many are not aware that the average voter has been described as "male, white, and middle class." It seems clear that political figures cannot ignore "middle class revolts" if they are to maintain themselves in office.

Urban renewal is one program which one might suppose would appeal both to the poor and to the middle class. Blighted downtown areas would be made more attractive to both groups, and the destruction of substandard housing would surely please the poor. But the wealthier groups often feel that such programs are a waste of money, and both the rich and the poor may miss familiar landmarks.

Urban renewal has often meant the destruction of buildings in a slum area, which has only pushed the slum dweller into a perhaps even less attractive slum in an area more remote from the center of the city and hence less desirable in location, as well. Some of the new apartment buildings which replace destroyed slum housing seem not to be designed with the needs of the poor in mind at all. Hotels, motels, civic centers, and convention centers arc built. City fathers always seem interested in attracting conventions, although it is likely to seem to the poor of the city that conventions are advantageous only to hotel and restaurant owners.

Sometimes attractive housing complexes are built in areas cleared by urban renewal, but these may be designed with middle class or upper middle class residents in mind. But it is to be hoped that the development of apartment buildings owned by the tenant can satisfy the desire and need of the middle class citizen to own the place in which he lives, without using enormous quantities of land, which is scarce near the center of a city and hence very valuable.

Some of the newer apartment complexes provide many of the

same benefits so forcefully advertised by the suburban developer. Thus, they often have swimming pools and recreational facilities. When the apartment complex provides a "party room," which can be reserved by one of the tenants for entertaining, the apartment dweller may very well find that he does not need as large a home as he would if he had to provide facilities for entertaining his friends within his own domicile. Therefore, he may find that he can live in an apartment with a smaller number of square feet than he would think necessary if he lived in a house in the suburbs. The fact remains, however, that the monthly payment for a house in the suburbs, including principal, interest, insurance, and taxes, is often very, very much less than the rent which must be charged for anything like equivalent living space in an apartment located in the city. However, some middle class families are finding the advantages of regular maintenance of both the apartment fixtures and the grounds to be worth some additional financial outlay.

Cities are now beginning to give attention to air pollution. Automobiles now have smog-control devices. Cities are now requiring that their industries give attention to what they put into the air of the city and the surrounding lakes and rivers. More and more, cities are giving greater attention to the development and maintenance of their parks and other recreational areas. Certainly, at its best, any really large city can provide museums, zoos, aquariums, and other cultural advantages which not even a large and prosperous suburb could hope to afford.

There are many urban problems, not all of which are directly related to the flight of the middle class. However, anything which makes the city more attractive and its facilities more available will tend to diminish this flight. Certainly, the development of rapid transit systems, which make it possible for citizens to move from one part of the city to another rapidly and economically, without the construction of more unsightly freeways which take more property off the tax rolls and without the necessity of bringing more and more automobiles into the center of the city, is long overdue. When city transportation facilities are inadequate, the worker is forced to use his automobile. Once in his automobile and on a freeway, usually the driver cares little whether he drives ten miles or twenty miles. And finally, hope-fully some way will be found to greatly decrease the amount of corruption within our cities, which is so often cited by those who uphold the rural virtues.

If there once was a battle between ruralism and urbanism in the United States, the battle is now over, and urbanism has won. We are going to live, most of us, at any rate, in enormous metropolitan areas. The question is only what a typical metro-politan area will be like. Will it be a vast, teeming slum, sur-rounded by wealthy suburbs, which are a part of the metropolitan area but yet remote from the city, or will it be a center of indus-try, commerce, culture, and recreation, surrounded by city homes as well as bedroom communities?

NOTES

[1]Patricia Sexton, *Education and Income* (New York: Viking, 1961), p. 120.

[2]Robert J. Havighurst, *The Public Schools of Chicago* (Board of Education of the City of Chicago, 1964), p. 175.

CHAPTER II

Learning in the Urban School

Since our largest cities are melting pots for persons of diverse ethnic, racial, and economic backgrounds, it may be expected that the students in a city school system will come to a school with many different cultural backgrounds. Particularly, students who attend schools in lower class neighborhoods may be expected to differ markedly from middle or upper class students who attend schools in the wealthier suburbs. Yet, the school curriculum and teaching methods in many schools seem designed with only the middle class student in mind. Although the central task of the school is to help each child master the fundamental skills of learning, it must also concern itself with the socialization of each child. The healthy growth, emotional as well as mental and physical, of every student should be one of the concerns of the school.

The school and those who run the school should be sensitive to the background and education of the parent and to the community or neighborhood in which both parent and student live. The parent must become involved with the school in such a way that he can understand the importance of education and take pride in the schools of his neighborhood. Particularly the lower class parent desperately needs support and reinforcement. Care must be taken not to bring shame to the parent by reason of his dress, his manner of speech, or the minority culture from which he is drawn.

Although the teacher is one of the central figures in the learning process, he has not come to terms with the background of the student as a problem with which he must deal. In general, the school has not been sensitive to the problems associated with the slum culture of the lower class student. The teacher has not

26

understood the lower class student's world—a world in which the middle class teacher does not himself live. The emphasis in our present educational system is to make the lower class student conform to middle class values.

The teacher, a mature, educated individual, assumes the task of bringing the lower class student up to the so-called standard. There is little attempt on the part of the school to utilize the experiences lower class children bring from their slum culture. The school often neglects to consider the influence of the slum street culture, the poverty, the crowded tenement houses, the language handicap, and all the other factors which contribute to dividing the slum children from their upper and middle class fellow students.

The greatest changes of all will have to occur in the attitudes and behavior of faculty members themselves. The most significant school activities are those which involve the faculty. The day-to-day actions of the faculty in the total educational program of school will indeed determine whether it will be successful or unsuccessful.

The lower class student in the big city comes to a middle class institution and is taught by a member of the middle class. It makes no difference whether or not the teacher was born into the lower class. He received entrance into the middle class along with his teaching certificate. Thus, by both the institution and the teacher, the lower class child is made to conform to middle class standards and accept middle class goals, regardless of the standards and goals accepted by his family and neighbors. Often the student is allowed no time to make a transition and is frequently given no assistance in making the transition to a new set of goals and values. This conflict begins to penalize the lower class student from his very first day at school.

Let us now examine the urban elementary school, and particularly the first grade, which, after all, is the real beginning of a child's academic experience. The rapid social and cultural changes which are taking place in urban industrial communities complicate the first-grader's adjustment at home and in the neighborhood and hence affect his psychosocial security as well as his ability to learn. That segmented character of urban life, which has become the dominant mode in American society, has resulted in the ascendancy of secondary over primary relationships, thus weakening the primary group structure—the family —and its controls. With urbanization have come social disorganization, insecurity, and family disintegration. The positive male image is rapidly disappearing from the American scene.

In many economically deprived families of our largest cities, the wife holds a more lucrative position than does her husband. Particularly is this the case in Mexican, Puerto Rican, and Negro families. The husband's identity as a breadwinner of the household, of course, is threatened. Thus, the young child is vulnerable to identity diffusion in his cultural environment, and his concepts of behavior appropriate to the sexes differs from the values and expectations of the community. His contact with the female teacher in the ghetto primary grades only reinforces his home experiences. It is usually not until the child reaches junior high school, and in some communities senior high school, that he is taught by a male teacher. In many instances, a traumatic crisis may arise over this new experience. Also, he is seldom taught by a member of a minority group.

At this point let us not forget the children of broken families, or those born out of wedlock, or those whose fathers are deceased. The child without a father figure in the home will be deprived of male leadership and direction in his early formative years. These youngsters need to have contact with both sexes in order to learn to alternate their modes of behavior in response to the sexes as well as to make a more wholesome adjustment in their adult lives. The male teacher can influence the child's feelings about learning by his own attitude and example. He can help the child view attainment of knowledge and school success as worthy activities. The security derived from the male teacher, especially if he is a member of a minority group, can well be a basic ingredient of academic learning for many culturally deprived, fatherless first-graders. The male's central importance in the classroom will be a visible sign to the child of the trustworthy and representative role he will play in the grown-up world—a world where he will be expected to take his place, as have all other children who have had the benefit of male exposure and companionship.

It is generally recognized that learning problems are more common among boys than girls, especially in reading. A young boy whose primary adult contacts consist of his mother and his female first-grade teacher may develop a faulty identification with the male sex and his father in particular. In essence, a poor masculine identification with the male sex and a distorted self-image may develop during those early formative years. Reading, school success, and even the teaching profession itself, in the eyes of the first-grader, may be equated with femininity. However, there are doubtless other explanations for the observed phenomenon that girls seem to do better than boys in school.

By the age of six a boy usually identifies with his father. However, if he has no model to imitate, perhaps he may find a masculine role awkward when circumstances place him in it. A balanced elementary school faculty needs a variety of personalities as well as men on its staff.[1]

The authors believe that one of the reasons for the rise in adolescent delinquency in the cities during the last two decades can be traced as far back as the first grade, where the kinds of men after whom boys should model themselves have been nonexistent. The lower grades need to provide the opportunity for male students to express their masculine qualities. There is a need for male teachers from minority groups, who can provide suitable models for boys to emulate and can challenge a boy's physical aptitude as well as his mental outlook. A boy needs to have a masculine idol. If he does not find one in school, he will turn to the streets, to the local gang, to the dope addict, or to the pool hall.

Here is one of the most critical problems the urban elementary schools face: the prospective male teacher wants no part of teaching first-graders. Conversely, the authors were horrified to learn that there is a belief in educational quarters that female teachers are inherently superior for this role. This attitude is as archaic as the horse and buggy on Madison Avenue. In a sense, teacher education in this country is at a crossroad; when and how shall we attract men to teach in the grades, especially at the primary level? There has been much progress in the last decade in teaching techniques and media, and there is the probability of much more in the decade ahead. However, there is an urgent need to make personnel changes in our schools in order to promote the healthy growth of our children. We shall, indeed, have passed up an almost incredible opportunity if we stand still on this issue.

The prestige of the urban elementary school must be raised, and its image altered in professional circles, if it is to attract qualified men. There is need for a concerted effort on the part of schools of education, placement officers, school boards, and school administrators to encourage prospective male candidates to teach in the elementary school. Such incentives as equal teaching loads with secondary schools, free preparation periods, and duty-free lunch hours merit serious consideration. The plain fact is that men will hesitate to teach in the lower grades unless the suggestions cited above are implemented and the cultural stigma of teaching younger children is erased.[2]

Another problem which socially disadvantaged children bring with them to school, besides the lack of adequate father figures, is the inability to speak and understand the middle class American English for their section of the country. The child so handicapped can neither understand his teacher nor make himself understood by his teacher. The language of a slum is often fully developed, with its own consistent grammar. The child must continue to use this language in order to maintain communication with his parents and neighbors while attempting to learn another language for use in school. Although the older immigrants had the same difficulty, their problem was more widely recognized and they were given assistance in meeting it.

In some of the large cities of the Southwest, particularly in San Antonio, Texas, are found some of the worst slums in the world. Here there are poverty and illiteracy to a greater extent than almost anywhere else. One of the greatest problems is language. The people speak neither English nor Spanish as taught in our schools, but rather a kind of Texas-Mexican Spanish dialect which is understandable to few Anglos. Many children from this area simply repeat the first grade until they begin to understand a little of the English spoken by the teacher. In many schools, instruction in Spanish is prohibited, and is encouraged only in a few schools, on a small scale.[3]

Differences in language are quite obvious in San Antonio, but the difference can also cause trouble in New York and other cities. Puerto Ricans in New York have a similar problem, but so do the Negroes of New York slums. Of course, the child must learn to speak and understand the language of the school, but some accommodation could be made to his needs during a transitional period. And we should expect the teacher to learn to understand the native dialect of his students.

Even in situations where the language barrier is less important, the middle class first-grader is likely to have a far larger vocabulary than does the lower class first-grader. The middle class first-grader has spent hours watching television. His parents have probably taken him on more than one trip, so that he has a larger background of experiences. He may have seen farms, waterfalls, lakes, the mountains, or the ocean, all before he ever comes to school. He has almost certainly attended kindergarten, even in states which do not provide free public kindergartens. He may even have attended a private nursery school from the age of three. Such advantages cost money. Middle class parents have the money and the educational background to value such programs. Lower class parents usually have neither.

Middle class preschool children get a lot more attention from their parents. If a lower class child has the advantage of living with both parents, both his mother and father are more likely than are middle class parents to be employed. Many middle class children reach the first grade able to write their names and count, and they are often able to read. Such accomplishments are rare among lower class children, who are sometimes several years behind, so to speak, before they even enter first grade.

The Head Start program was founded in an attempt to deal with this problem. Unfortunately, the program has not been on a large enough scale in many parts of the country to have had much effect. Furthermore, there is some middle class opposition. Some Negro leaders have called for a massive program beginning with four-year-old children in order to bring deprived children up to first-grade level before they start first grade. Not much has been done to implement this suggestion.

In Charlotte, North Carolina, it was found that Negro students entering junior high school were so far behind in reading and arithmetic that they had no hope of coping with the curriculum. In order to prevent this situation from perpetuating itself, a remedial program for fifth- and sixth-grade students was established after school, sponsored by a church congregation. The program was staffed by volunteers, including some college students in a teacher education program. All those who participated were surprised by the eagerness to learn evidenced by the students. Discipline was easily maintained by the simple threat that those who did not behave might not be allowed to stay after school to learn arithmetic and reading.

The attention span of the students was short, and many volunteers were needed: at least one "teacher" for each six students. But the students did show that they could learn and that they were interested in learning. Unfortunately, the program was not funded and finally had to be abandoned.

In some parts of the country, lower class children are not able to learn because they are hungry. The thirty cents charged by some school cafeterias may seem very reasonable to middle class parents, but it is often beyond the means of some families, especially those with several children in school. Where schools have been able to provide free lunches, and even free breakfasts in some cases, it has been found that the interest in learning and even the intelligence quotient of some students improved. Why are not free lunch and free breakfast programs more common in our schools? The school, being a middle class institution, with middle class teachers and administrators, is not equipped to deal with the situation at present. Many do not even know that such problems exist.

What of the textbooks used by school children? Are they written with the needs of all school children in mind? Alas, they are usually written by middle class authors for middle class suburban children to read about middle class situations. The pictures in these books are of nice homes on nice, quiet tree-shaded streets. They show children playing with bicycles, wagons, and other toys, all new and shiny. They show mothers working in big, clean, modern kitchens and fathers going off to work in business suits, often carrying brief cases. The child who lives in East Harlem, New York City, for example, does not see in his textbook a picture of a building which reminds him of the one in which he lives, crowded, dirty, and in poor repair. He sees no pictures of buildings with fire escapes, garbage, clothes lines, dirty streets and alleys. He sees no pictures of anything which help him to visualize his life. On the other hand, the middle class pupil is also deprived of an opportunity to "see how the other half lives," to use the phrase used by Jacob Riis in his classic work, *How the Other Half Lives*, written at the turn of the century.

Even the problems in elementary school arithmetic texts must read very strangely to the urban slum dweller. Consider this one: "John and Mary's father wants to construct a patio which will open off the family room of their home. If the dimensions of the patio are to be 12 feet by 10 feet, how many ten inch tiles will be needed?" As an arithmetic problem, this is fairly standard and not too difficult. But some of the children may wonder what a patio is or even what a family room is. Also, why not "build" instead of "construct"? Why not "stones" instead of "tiles"? But above all, why not a problem having to do with an apartment building in a city, rather than one that surely deals with a home in the suburbs?

When educational films are shown in the school, the picture of the home which is presented is certainly very foreign to many of the students. The people are all too well dressed. Why not a picture of "Daddy" wearing overalls and carrying a lunch pail? Why not a picture of a tenement or at least an apartment building, rather than a picture of a home in the suburbs? Certainly, city children need to see pictures of suburbs and even of farms and farm animals, but surely not to the exclusion of all that is familiar. Should not education proceed from the known to the unknown?

The vocabulary of the youth of the central city is not used in either text or classroom. Words such as *stick, fire escape, tar roof, back alley*, and many others seldom appear in the primers of the lower grades or even the upper grades; yet these are the realities to the child of the slum. These are the tools of articulation for the lower class child, but they are ignored in both textbooks and classrooms. Instead, the texts teach words that describe pleasant situations—words which the slum child will seldom use and are seldom used by his associates. Admittedly some publishers have attempted to provide textbooks with which deprived and minority children could identify. However, in sections of the country where newly integrated Negro children most need to be able to identify with their school situation, the textbooks appear to be designed to please the white power structure rather than to achieve a sound educational purpose.

Clearly, there is a real need to build on the foundation which these children take with them to the school. Their formal education must begin at the point which circumstances have permitted them to reach. In teaching these children, then, use must be made of the vocabulary which they already have. Words which the children already know can be used in the classroom, even if these words are not part of Thorndyke's ten thousand. What is so sacred about Thorndyke's ten thousand words, anyway? To ignore the words and situations which are already a part of a student's culture in favor of words and situations foreign to his experience is to make education irrelevant and meaningless to the student. Is it surprising that the student to whom the school is irrelevant should become a dropout?

New textbooks will have to be written for the use of the ghetto school child, but much can be accomplished with present audiovisual materials and techniques. The culturally deprived child by his very nature must be stimulated for learning through direct experiences. As Ray states, "Some of the learning problems of children who fit into the category often labeled 'culturally deprived' will be lessened if their experience background is enlarged and enriched through selected visual and aural experiences."[4] The teacher of the lower class child must be able to select and effectively use technology which will supply the experiences necessary for the particular child's development and growth. Modern technology can provide a wide range of materials for the selection of the teacher. Films, filmstrips, slides, tapes, mimeographed materials, projectors, and the newer members of the teaching media field, television and teaching machines, can make possible the development of a learning environment suitable for the culturally deprived child.

It is only when the school recognizes that it is in the area of language development that the culturally underprivileged child manifests the greatest degree of intellectual retardation will the educational programs for these children be meaningfully developed around the visual and auditory experiences they can understand. What the teacher needs to know is what hardware and software to select and how to use them effectively.

In addition to problems in urban elementary schools, there are also problems in urban secondary schools, where the multiplicity of programs and disciplines represented tends to compound difficulties. Clearly the more limited vocabulary of the lower class student continues to cause trouble in English classes. In literature classes it is clear that the materials used are chosen more to prepare middle class students for college entrance examinations than to interest the average urban-dwelling student. There is now an abundance of good literature which deals with urban problems. We may hope that some of this literature can find its way into the high school English class. But rather than discuss the difficulties encountered in the study of each individual discipline, let us examine in depth the secondary school mathematics curriculum as it affects the urban student.

When a student reaches the ninth grade, his academic road forks, at least as far as mathematics is concerned. He may take either algebra or something called general mathematics, ninth-grade mathematics, or, more rarely, commercial algebra or commercial arithmetic. This division is not to be compared with ability grouping in English or history, as the material taught in algebra is very different from the subject matter of general mathematics. The difference is not merely in standards, or in intensity, but in actual content. This fork in the academic road is uniquely mathematical. Doubtless the college-bound student is more likely to enroll in physics, chemistry, or Latin and the noncollege-bound student more likely to enroll in machine shop or commercial subjects, but there is no separation within any of these disciplines.

Until about thirty years ago there was no question that general mathematics was for the weaker student, however determined. General mathematics was sometimes called "bonehead math" or by other equally derogatory epithets. The selection of students for general mathematics, as opposed to algebra, was based on grades in seventh- and eighth-grade arithmetic, on intelligence test scores, and sometimes on scores in reading tests. Often the selection was also based on the status of the parents in the community. Enrollment in algebra in the ninth grade became a status symbol. The son of the banker, the lawyer, or the doctor could not be compelled to enroll in general mathematics, regardless of his intelligence or his grades in previous mathematics courses. His parents would not understand why he could not take algebra.

Sometimes the student who completed general mathematics in a highly satisfactory manner would be able to enroll in algebra in the tenth grade, but such a student was extremely rare in most high schools. Although intelligence and skill in arithmetic were regarded as prerequisite to algebra, the relative certainty of eventually attending a college or university was a more important criterion. Therefore, the social and economic status of the parents became highly important. Thus, even a student who had completed general mathematics and done well would not necessarily be more likely to attend college. Most educators do not like to admit that this dichotomy of the ninth-grade mathematics student body into the bright, socially elite, and college-bound on the one hand and the dull, deprived, and blue collar type on the other still exists.

The two courses, we are told, are designed to serve students with different needs. Presumably, the college-bound student would need to know algebra, particularly if he hoped to be an engineer or a scientist. The noncollege-bound student would need no algebra, but would instead need to have information about insurance, annuities, installment purchases, taxes, loans and mortgages, and the like. Why it is felt that such information would be superfluous for the college-bound student is indeed not clear.

The problem of separation of students does not end in the ninth grade. Students who successfully complete algebra in the ninth grade usually take geometry in the tenth grade. A second year of algebra is offered in the eleventh grade, and this is now demanded for admission to most of the better colleges and universities. But in some large cities, students are not permitted to enroll in second-year algebra unless they made a grade of B in first-year algebra. At least one school administration claims any student who has failed to made a grade of B in first-year algebra would be certain to fail second-year algebra. However, further examination reveals that this regulation does not apply equally to all students. If the parents are influential in the community, the student may enroll in second-year algebra even if he received C or D in first-year algebra.

The time has come for curriculum constructors and classroom teachers to begin to ask if mathematics should be used as a vehicle to differentiate our middle class, college-bound students from the urban poor. It is terribly frightening to find that a division of a discipline has been made to correspond to and hence to help perpetuate class distinction.[5]

One means by which curricular-determined class distinctions could be eliminated or, at least, minimized is effective guidance and counseling programs. Although often ignored or overlooked, guidance and counseling can and should be an integral part of the total learning situation. Counseling is necessary not only to enable the child of the slum to relate to the school situation but also to assist him with the problem of relating to the world in which he must live and work after he has left school.

Schools must provide more and better-trained guidance counselors. Guidance counselors ought not to be solely advisers on colleges for students who are college-bound. Many school administrators today are demanding more guidance counselors, but not all of them are thinking of persons trained to counsel and advise the poor and disadvantaged students.

Since many students attending specialized high schools in our large urban centers are forced in their adolescence to make some kind of occupational choice, it is imperative that they be given an adequate introduction to occupations and above all a realistic picture of the labor market. Because occupational choices are increasingly being made in the school, remote from many of the realities of the world of work, it is necessary that the students who are planning to terminate their formal schooling upon completion of high school be given as much, or even more, attention than students who plan to continue their education beyond high school. Counseling is often directed at the college-bound students and quite frequently neglects two other groups: students who will enter the labor market after graduation, and potential dropouts. Students who could benefit from some form of post-high-school education other than college are also neglected and not informed of the opportunities available to them.

The selection of an occupation not only may determine whether one will be employed or unemployed, successful or unsuccessful, but also will influence almost every other aspect of one's life. During the next decade, the school counselor will be called upon to assist an unprecedented number of students to make intelligent career choices. The greatest problem of occupational choice will arise from automation and the changes in the employment market.

There is little doubt in the minds of educators that the counseling personnel, in spite of the contributions of the National Defense Education Act institutes and other specialized programs, will not be adequate to meet the educational and vocational needs of the urban student population. It is with this thought in mind that the authors believe that occupational information can be best disseminated within the existing capabilities through the classrooms. Several questions now arise: What are some of the opportunities for learning about the world of work which the group method provides? How can the group method be used to bring the world of work to the classroom?

First and foremost, the group method of presenting occupational information can serve as a vehicle for transmitting many pertinent facts and points of general interest to the student. For example, contacts with professional people, skilled tradesmen, and managerial personnel can be made within the range of the classroom through the group technique. Second, the group technique can serve to stimulate critical thinking about occupations in the minds of many students who otherwise would not be prompted to these considerations. This is especially true of students living in low socioeconomic areas who have limited opportunity to be exposed to the multitude of occupations that exist outside their daily experience. Sociological factors affect occupational choice by limiting the occupations with which the student is acquainted. Form and Miller point out that the social world in which the student lives can exclude opportunity and limit his career aspirations.[6] The student obviously can make a choice only among the occupations with which he is familiar.

Cuony and Hoppock, who are leading students of occupational information, undertook to determine whether or not the group method of disseminating occupational information would produce amelioration of an individual's learning power and job satisfaction.[7] Cuony taught a course, "Job Finding and Job Orientation," to an experimental group of high school seniors. He compared the experimental group, in terms of job satisfaction and earning power, with an equated control group not given occupational information. The combined annual earnings of the experimental group exceeded those of the control group by $7,719. Job satisfaction was found to be more prevalent among the members of the experimental group than among those of the control group. There was less unemployment among the pupils in the experimental group than among those in the control group.

Four years after the first study was made, Cuony again compared the same experimental group and control group used in his first experiment.[8] The average pupil in the experimental group was earning $3,105 per year, while the pupils in the control group were averaging $2,614 per year. The combined earnings of the experimental group exceeded those of the control group for the same year by $14,226. The entire cost of the course to the school was $1,542.

Through the group technique it is possible to introduce students to a wide breadth of occupations so that needs and interests of the students can be met. The group atmosphere, unlike individual counseling, gives the students an excellent opportunity to share with their classmates their feelings, attitudes, and experiences about their career aspirations. This is one of the most promising areas for a counselor to explore with his students. A genuine healthy give-and-take about occupations will give deprived students more information as well as help them explore and interpret the material that is exchanged in the classroom.

Many educators are recognizing that the years prior to high school—even the elementary school years—represent the period when the selection of careers should begin to crystallize in the minds of students. Our schools need to plan occupational programs which are realistic, informative, and available to all the students. The dissemination of occupational information should not be limited to the very infrequent personal interviews between counselor and student which are held once or twice a year for a twenty- or thirty-minute period. It should involve a concerted effort throughout the school year to assure student growth toward maturity in understanding the world of work.

Certainly an opportunity should be afforded a student who wishes to learn a trade in high school. But in many cities the vocational or technical high schools are simply the dumping grounds where the citizens of the lowest social class are allowed to deposit their children. Sometimes "shops" are to be found in a regular high school, usually hidden in some corner of the basement, as though this part of the curriculum were contaminated. A new look must be taken at the role of vocational and technical training in our secondary schools.

The problems of learning in urban schools are many and varied and require a many-pronged attack if they are to be solved. We propose changes in the ethnic and racial make-up of the teaching staff of urban schools and in the male-female ratio in urban elementary school faculties. We propose changes in the texts, films, and other educational media used in urban schools, so that the total learning experience will have more relation to life as lived by the majority of the pupils. We propose a curriculum fair to all the students, regardless of their social or economic status. We propose literature courses which include Negro and Latin American literature and history courses which include the contributions of Negroes and Latin Americans. And finally, we propose greatly expanded guidance and counseling services for urban youth.

But clearly the education which each pupil receives depends in large measure on the attitudes and vision of his teachers as well as on their knowledge. Where will the teachers needed by our urban schools be found, where trained, and how rewarded?

NOTES

[1]Lee J. Cronbach, *Educational Psychology* (New York: Harcourt, Brace, 1954), pp. 316-318.

[2]Philip D. Vairo, "Wanted: 20,000 Male First Grade Teachers." Reprinted from the February/March 1969 issue of *Education*. Copyright 1969 by The Bobbs-Merrill Company, Inc., Indianapolis, Indiana.

[3]For further information on the language problem in Texas, see *The Texas Observer,* June 9, 1967, pp. 30-31.

[4]Henry W. Ray, "Environment-Enrichment Program in Pennsylvania," *Audio-Visual Instruction,* X (January, 1965), 35.

[5]William M. Perel and Philip D. Vairo, "What is General Mathematics?" *Journal of Secondary Education,* XXXXII (March, 1968), 109-113.

[6]William Form and Delbert Miller, *Industrial Sociology* (New York: Harper, 1951), pp. 728-729.

[7]Edward Cuony and Robert Hoppock, "Job Course Pays Off," *Personnel and Guidance Journal,* XXXII (March, 1954), 389.

[8]Edward Cuony and Robert Hoppock, "Job Course Pays Off Again," *Personnel and Guidance Journal,* XXXVI (October, 1957), 116.

CHAPTER III

The Training and Recruitment of Teachers for Urban Schools

Probably no other problem is causing more confusion and anxious moments than the one of determining the type of faculty that is needed to teach in our cities and the kind of training which these faculty members should receive if they are going to function effectively. Teachers should be carefully selected and should have many opportunities for inservice training in curricular problems and, perhaps more important, in problems of human relations and uncovering and developing academic talent.

Big city schoolteachers are products of rather standardized preservice and inservice teacher training programs, which in essence reflect the mores and traditions of the past. The teacher training institution presents certain perceptions of the ghetto from the standpoint of professors, who in reality have been removed from this social phenomenon. Although some university professors are making many positive contributions to work in the ghettos of our cities, they hold many significant negative attitudes. These negative attitudes are more frequently caused by a lack of understanding of the problems of teaching in a ghetto school than by some basis of valid criticism. A further complication is the fact that big city teachers, especially ghetto schoolteachers, often lack the status within the profession which is accorded to teachers in the suburbs. The university professor himself may gain more status by preparing teachers who will teach in schools which serve middle or upper class youth. Ours is a status-conscious society, and no one can pretend that teachers and professors are never guilty of what has been called "status striving."

An over-all assessment of teacher education programs is needed in order to prepare teachers adequately to work intelligently with lower class students. There is a definite need to expose prospective teachers to the implications of the civil rights movement and Negro and Hispanic history and culture. Positive attitudes must be developed toward our citizens from the lower socioeconomic strata of our society. No longer can we ignore the idea of meeting the needs of the underprivileged, Negro and white, in our teacher training institutions. Our students must receive the proper preparation in order to ensure that they will be ready to meet this challenge.

If the interested prospective teacher tries to learn about teaching in a ghetto from his textbooks, he is apt to be disappointed. The textbook authors, like the authors of the scholarly books, are usually not experienced in teaching in central city schools. In many methods courses and texts, problems of teaching the socially disadvantaged, the poor, and the slow learner are seldom mentioned or inadequately treated. When methods courses are divided by discipline, most of the attention is devoted to the courses taken by the college-bound. For example, in mathematics the prospective teacher is likely to learn about geometry, trigonometry, and various things called either "advanced math" or "modern math." The problem of what to do with the general mathematics student who cannot do the arithmetic expected of fifth-grade students is not mentioned. Furthermore, prospective English teachers are not taught methods useful to them in dealing with high school students who read at the fifth-grade level. They are not taught methods which would aid them in making *Hamlet* and *Paradise Lost* or *Leaves of Grass* relevant either to a New York slum student or to a North Carolina rural student.

The professors of education who teach the prospective teacher may or may not be interested in the problems of urban education; and, if interested, they are rarely able to offer much help. The professors may have had no contact with lower class students and no teaching experience in urban elementary or secondary schools. A severe problem exists in southern cities, where prospective white teachers, now faced with the problem of teaching in integrated schools, are still taught almost entirely by white professors whose public school experience was gained during the days of segregation. James B. Conant has called repeatedly for the use of clinical professors who have firsthand and, most of all, up-to-date teaching experience. The alternative is either to do nothing or to ask that the blind lead the blind.

Incredible as it may seem, the authors have found that professors in other disciplines who have had teaching experience in urban elementary and secondary schools often seek to keep it hidden, fearing loss of status within the academic community. There is obviously no valid reason why a faculty member with experience and training in urban schoolwork should not be willing to admit to such experience and to make his training and experience available to the teacher education program. There is equally no valid reason why a professor in another discipline, who is involved with the training of prospective teachers in subject matter, should not have at least as much contact with ghetto elementary and secondary schools as could be obtained by an occasional visit to a school, perhaps to assist the education faculty in observing student teachers in his discipline. However, most academic professors would react negatively to such proposals, which may in part explain why professors of education have not taken the initiative in demanding that their administrations establish postdoctoral internships for them in elementary and secondary schools. Professors, in general, even go so far as to differentiate themselves professionally from their colleagues in the public schools.[1]

Unfortunately, by differentiating himself and isolating himself from elementary and secondary school teachers, the university professor often fails to take an interest in the teacher training function of his institution. Even many professors of education are not involved with the training of teachers for ghetto schools, nor do they very often want to be involved. Since professors of education have often been the scapegoats of the academic faculty, sometimes justly so, they have tended to play down the practical aspect of their teaching experience and focus their attention on the so-called theoretical questions of the day. As an education professor gains experience and rises in rank and seniority at his institution, there is a tendency for him to become further and further removed from the preservice training role of his institution and to become more and more involved with specialized course work in philosophy, history of education, counseling, educational psychology, school administration, school social work, and so on.

One of the major criticisms launched against teacher training programs of urban universities is that the personnel instructing the student teachers have had little or no teaching experience during the past five or ten years on the level for which they are supposedly preparing teachers. This is especially true of college instructors preparing students to teach in ghetto schools. Certainly, as a minimum qualification, we should demand that the professor return to full-time teaching, at the grade levels at which he prepares teachers, for at least one semester every five or six years. The professor should serve as an exchange colleague or as a visiting teacher in an urban elementary or secondary school, with his salary supplemented by his college or university, so that this exchange program would entail no financial sacrifice on his part.

During this semester, the college professor should be actively involved in observation and interclass visitations in the school at which he is obtaining his inservice experience. Teachers in the school should have opportunities to meet with him and discuss problems of mutual concern. He should have an opportunity to observe demonstration lessons given by the more experienced teachers and supervisory personnel in the school. New media and teaching innovations should be introduced to the professor during his tenure at the school. Most of all, he should be encouraged to experiment and attempt to implement new ideas and practices in his daily lessons. In essence, on-the-job, inservice training should be a real and meaningful experience for the college professor.

Learning about teaching in the urban ghetto is no substitute for actual classroom experience! The Conant demand for clinical professors, mentioned earlier, can no longer be ignored. It is not at all uncommon for the college professor to have been away from classroom teaching for more than fifteen years. It is easy to see why the student teacher may find it difficult to accept advice and criticism from the college professor, whom he cannot respect professionally.

Yet, the very colleges and universities that are engaged in educating teachers provide no relief, so that the college professor can return to the public school. Sabbatical leaves are seldom, if ever, available for this purpose. Even if they were, most professors would probably rather use their sabbaticals for purposes other than obtaining fresh experience in precollege teaching. Institutions not offering sabbaticals to their staffs—and there is a large number of such institutions—have not, to our knowledge, initiated plans whereby education faculty members could return to urban elementary or secondary schools without substantial loss in salary. In no real sense can a professor of education give attention to the problem of improving his knowledge of teaching techniques at the elementary and secondary levels, and broadening his horizons, while teaching a full load of courses at his college or university.

Before we can develop expert teachers to deal effectively with the educational problems of our day, we are going to need to expose more of our college staff to up-to-date teaching experiences in our schools. The National Education Association, in a recent study, pointed out three areas in which teachers were found lacking in their preparation.[2] These are (1) teaching methods (24 percent); (2) classroom management routines and discipline (38 percent); and (3) use of audiovisual equipment and materials (49 percent). All three of these areas are directly related to the instruction prospective teachers received by the teacher education faculty. It can be readily recognized that the three areas mentioned above, because of their very nature, require recent teaching experience on the part of the college professor.

The preparation of teachers for our larger cities is indeed one of the most pressing problems facing our colleges and universities. The National Council on Education for the Disadvantaged recently singled out the attitudes of teachers as the crucial ingredient in success or failure in teaching socially disadvantaged youth. Only by actual contact with the children of the poor can the professor readily appreciate their problems and be able to share his experience with his own students. The professor must recognize that the children of poverty in the urban ghettos have special problems and special needs. It is insufficient to just read about their problems in professional literature, for very frequently the very authors who purport to be experts on these problems have themselves never taught in a school serving the children of the poor, as we have already indicated.

The middle class status of the teacher has been the subject of much comment, mostly unfavorable. But a great deal of what is written on this subject puts too much emphasis on what must be done to assist the prospective teacher to overcome his middle class prejudices and obtain knowledge and understanding of the disadvantaged. If teachers in the elementary and secondary schools are middle class, surely the professors in the colleges and universities which train the teachers are middle class or higher. Too little emphasis has been placed on their understanding of the problem of the disadvantaged. Professors of education, who themselves lack the necessary experience with or knowledge of the problems of urban society, are preparing prospective teachers for urban schools. These teachers, in turn, will not be prepared to teach the children of the poor. We must think in terms of programs to prepare adequately those who will teach the future teachers for our urban schools.

The education faculty of at least some urban universities is attempting to meet the challenge. Dr. James E. Allen, United States Commissioner of Education, while Commissioner of Education for the State of New York, called upon the colleges and universities of New York to plan teacher education programs to meet the needs of urban youth. Fordham University is now attempting to develop new preservice and inservice programs for the preparation of urban teachers. These programs stress on-the-job training for teachers, but always with guidance, support, and supervision from the university, the schools, or both, to whatever extent necessary to guarantee competent teaching. Connections between theory and practice and the relationships among various phases of education are stressed. For example, educational psychology and methods of teaching are taught as two phases of the same process rather than as independent courses studied at different times. Also, the kinds of co-opera-

tive preservice and on-the-job teacher education activities designed to lead to continuing professional growth of both school
and university personnel are provided. In addition to the resources usually available in teacher education programs, the resources in many disciplines within the university are utilized.
Fordham University rejects the outworn concept that the competence of a beginning teacher can be developed by a lock-step
progression through a series of unrelated courses. Instead, the
procedures are adjusted to individual differences among teachers
as they develop skill in teaching.

Other urban universities have established such programs.
Wichita State University has established a pilot program in
which students serve as apprentices or teachers' aides in ghetto
schools long before they undertake the student teaching experience. When the prospective teacher is given such experience in
an actual school, problems of classroom management and discipline become real. The college student will demand real solutions
to such problems from his education professors and not be satisfied with theoretical or academic answers.

Difficult as is the problem of preparing teachers, especially
for urban schools, another problem is presented by the growing
complexity of the curriculum, particularly in the elementary
school. Today, we find that the subject matter of fifth-and sixth-
grade science and mathematics is much more advanced and
difficult to teach than were the science and mathematics of the
secondary school not long ago. Also, the curriculum of the fifth
and sixth grade is as diverse as was that of the junior high school.
The elementary school curriculum no longer consists entirely
of the three R's, but of social studies, science, and even foreign
languages, as well. The idea of the specialist, as opposed to the
generalist teacher, in the secondary school has long been accepted. Also, specialist teachers are used at all grade levels in
such fields as music, art, physical education, and now in foreign
languages. But there is a naive underlying assumption that the
elementary school teacher who has completed a course of study
within a school of education has sufficient competence to teach
advanced and specialized courses in such subjects as mathematics
and science to fifth-and sixth-graders. Students in the ghetto

schools need to be taught by competent teachers if they are to overcome the handicaps of their ghetto residence.

The authors recognize that the strongest argument for the generalist is that he will be able to provide continuity in the learning experiences of the pupils during their most formative years in school. In 1966, the authors served as consultants in a Comprehensive Improvement Project, sponsored by the State of North Carolina to assist culturally deprived first-grade students in a small southern city. An experimental design was established providing departmentalization according to the strengths and interests of the teachers involved in the project. Contrary to expectation, these teachers reacted very favorably to subject departmentalization, although they had all been teaching twenty or more years as elementary school generalists. The claim that it is impossible to get acquainted with every student, as a subject-matter specialist, was found invalid by these teachers. On the contrary, they expressed the feeling that it is impossible to do an effective job of teaching when one is responsible for subjects he is not prepared to teach.

We propose departmentalized instruction in the fifth and sixth grades. Of necessity, this change imposes on the teacher training institutions the task of preparing teachers in each of the subject-matter areas which comprise the fifth- and sixth-grade curriculums. The problems of teaching in an urban elementary school are sufficiently complex without demanding that a teacher attempt to handle material in which his training is less than adequate and with which he does not feel comfortable.

When teachers are adequately or even ideally trained for urban teaching, the problem of persuading them to accept appointments at ghetto schools remains. There is a need for prospective teachers to have a crusading zeal for the task of helping the socially underprivileged child. Haubrich reported several reasons why prospective teachers in New York City did not volunteer to teach in special service junior high schools for culturally deprived students.[3] They are:

1. "My parents wouldn't let me, and I would be afraid to walk through the neighborhood."
2. "I plan to teach in the suburbs."

3. "The discipline and reading problems would be too much for me to handle."

For a long time, American Negroes have needed to develop a sense of group identity and pride in their racial and cultural origins. Therefore, in the opinion of the authors, something like the present Black Power Movement is an absolute necessity. However, the Black Power Movement, particularly in its more militant aspects, has not helped the recruitment of white teachers for the schools of Negro ghettos in our large cities. In fact, some of its leaders do not even want black children taught by white teachers. Thus, there may be an increase in the number of white teachers leaving the ghetto schools of our cities. If this exodus becomes a reality, there may soon be a critical shortage of experienced personnel in our central city schools.

If we are going to attract and hold qualified teachers for our ghetto schools, the teacher's need for status and security cannot be overlooked. The teacher's relationship with the community and his identification as an equal partner with his peers in Scarsdale and Shaker Heights in the teaching profession are powerful forces. Incentives must be provided whereby teachers are persuaded to remain in ghetto schools for a reasonable period. Teacher turnover must be reduced if continuity of programs is to be achieved. Members of the minorities that inhabit the ghettos must be recruited for the teaching profession in far larger numbers than is presently the case. Career ladder opportunities must be made available to the paraprofessionals who work in ghetto schools and live in the immediate community.

For many reasons, then, teachers who are able and willing to teach in urban schools, particularly in ghetto schools, are in short supply. To gain insight into this shortage, it might be well to look at another situation in which a shortage of teachers creates a problem.

Many secondary school mathematics teachers are not really qualified to teach mathematics. The reason is simple: persons really qualified in mathematics are scarce, and many of those who are qualified choose not to enter the teaching profession. In recruiting mathematics teachers, school boards find themselves facing keen competition from businesses and governmental agencies who are trying to hire the same people. Such competition in salary and fringe benefits is not faced when social studies or English teachers are recruited. In 1964 the National Education Association Research Division made a study of the shortage of teachers in certain areas. It was found that mathematics was the most critical area, in terms of the new supply of teachers as a percent of demand.[4] The supply of new mathematics teachers represents only 80 percent of the demand, so that 20 percent of the teachers hired to teach mathematics are not prepared. The law of supply and demand operates in all other areas of our economy. It is no secret that our colleges and universities pay higher salaries to their mathematics faculty members than to their English or history faculty members. If many colleges and universities paid their mathematics professors the same salaries they pay their history professors, the qualifications of the mathematics professors would be greatly inferior to those of the history professors. Would this be fair to the students?

College and universities administrations have decided, by and large, that it is not fair and have made the decision to meet the demands of the market. Economists have been teaching us for years that salaries, as well as prices, are market-determined. Whether we like it or not, the market indicates a greater demand—and hence a higher price—on the services of mathematicians than on the services of persons in many other fields.

The shortage of teachers for ghetto schools may be just as acute as or even more acute than the shortage of mathematics teachers. Certainly, very few teachers have been trained specifically to teach in ghetto schools. Although every teacher training institution, particularly those in New York City, claims to have initiated programs specifically designed to train ghetto schoolteachers, these programs have not produced a substantial number of adequately trained teachers. Also, there is no guarantee that even an adequately trained ghetto school teacher will choose to teach in a ghetto school. The attractions of suburbia and of middle class schools have their effect on all teachers, regardless of their training. It is tragic that young persons ideally trained to be secondary school mathematics teachers may seek jobs in industry and never teach at all; but it is also tragic that even teachers specifically trained to teach in ghetto schools may feel the same need for middle class school status as teachers not so trained.

We propose the same solution for the shortage of ghetto teachers as for the shortage of mathematics teachers. If the supply is short, the price must be higher. If schools in urban ghettos cannot compete with schools in middle class neighborhoods for the available supply of teachers, a salary differential must be paid to ghetto teachers. Although the city school board will have some form of salary scale, based on experience, degrees, and so on, additional salary, perhaps in the form of a bonus or lightened teaching load not exceeding fifteen hours per week, could be given to each teacher in certain neighborhood areas. Class size should be held to a maximum of twenty. These steps not only would make teaching more desirable, pleasant, and even effective of itself but would give the ghetto teacher more status in the teaching profession. Probably additional funds, either to lighten teaching loads or to pay bonuses, would have to be provided by the state. Even the salary scale itself could be modified so as to make it possible to reward good teaching within the scale. There is no reason to continue the pattern whereby even a mediocre principal must be paid more than a superior teacher.

The problem of finding teachers of sufficient quality and quantity will continue to plague urban schools. As educators become aware that new methods of training urban teachers are needed, the new methods will be developed. We shall not continue the patterns of teacher education which were appropriate for the rural American society of the last century. As urban teachers gain status and professional rewards, they will surely become more plentiful. State departments of education and legislatures are becoming aware that a problem exists. The means of solution can and must be discovered.

NOTES

[1] See William M. Perel and Philip D. Vairo, "Professor, Is Your Experience Outdated?" *Educational Forum*, XXXIII (November, 1968), 39–44, for additional comment.

[2]Hazel Davis, "Profile of the American Public School Teacher, 1966," *NEA Journal,* LVI (May, 1967), 12.

[3]Vernon Haubrich, "The Culturally Different: New Context for Teacher Education," *Journal of Teacher Education*, XXI (June, 1963), 164–165.

[4]*NEA Research Bulletin* 42, (December, 1964), 122.

CHAPTER IV

Neighborhood Leadership for Urban Schools

In the United States, local control of education has always been considered a virtue. In contrast to the American system, most European countries have established national standards for curriculum and faculty to which the schools in all parts of the country must conform. Perhaps the European system is due to the more homogeneous population or to the older and more established societal structure. However, the federal framework with the concept of states' rights has played an important part in the development and pattern of American public education.

The free public school is an American innovation. From colonial days, new settlers in America have sought to establish schools and churches in their new communities almost as soon as they began to build houses and businesses. When Americans moved west and founded new towns after the Homestead Act was passed, they immediately established schools, which they controlled. These early settlers, who became farmers and ranchers, had little formal education. Yet, they hired the schoolteachers and established the standards and policies for their schools. Although the federal government encouraged education at all levels, even very early in our history, with the Morrill Act and in other ways, the control of education was invariably left with the states or local communities. Even today, where federal aid to schools has approached enormous proportions, the federal government has not sought and has not gained control of school systems. Accusations of federal control are sometimes made because of recent Supreme Court decisions and civil rights laws affecting school integration; but in matters of curriculum, faculty qualifications, and school plants, the federal government has imposed no requirements and has even failed to establish any national standards.

Public schools in the United States are typically creatures of the states. There is usually a state superintendent of public instruction as the titular head of the public schools in a state, and there is usually a state school board. Certification requirements for both teachers and school administrators are determined at the state level. A state may also establish standards for curriculum and physical facilities. But the day-to-day functioning of each school district is in the hands of a local board. The local board, even in a very small town with a school system involving only a few hundred students, is empowered to hire and fire teachers and administrators, to recommend taxes, to build or abandon school buildings, and to decide whether the curriculum shall be oriented toward college preparation or vocational training or both.

Small communities often lack persons of sufficient educational qualifications to serve on a school board charged with such important responsibilities, but such persons as are available do serve on school boards and exercise the powers described above. Stories of wealthy rural farmers sitting on school boards and asking prospective teachers whether or not they smoke, drink, or attend church, instead of dealing with more professional qualifications, are part of American educational folklore. Yet, no one seriously proposes that a small town should not run its schools through a locally elected school board just because the town lacks educated citizens.

In rural America there is a trend toward consolidation of school districts. If a district is too small, the per pupil expenditure becomes prohibitive in terms of services rendered. Also, too many teachers are required to teach outside their areas of specialization in small schools. Many small communities have resisted the trend toward school consolidation, but the movement of population from rural to urban areas forces consolidation to continue in spite of opposition. In urban areas, on the other hand, the citizens have begun to call for decentralization, and it is this demand which we propose to discuss.

Although those not acquainted with big city life may not realize it, a large city actually consists of a number of smaller communities. Each of these communities has its own shopping areas, schools, churches, recreational centers, and sometimes its own ethnic, racial, or religious characteristics. A resident of such a community may not often leave, even to go to the center of his city. He can shop, go to school and church, and often work within his own neighborhood. If he is a member of a non-English-speaking minority, he may fear to leave the neighborhood where his own language is spoken in the stores, the churches, and even by his supervisor at work. Other residents may see no need to leave, as the neighborhood is a complete community of itself.

Although called neighborhoods more often than communities, some "neighborhoods" have very large populations, even though they may encompass only a few city blocks. In cities in which the residents live in high-rise apartments, it is not difficult to find a neighborhood with a population not only exceeding that of small towns but even exceeding the populations of communities called cities. But the big city has only one school board for the schools of all its neighborhoods. Most big city school boards are appointed. However, Albert Shanker, President of the United Federation of Teachers, has recently proposed that the school board in New York be elected. On the other hand, the boards of many small towns have always been elected. In either case, minority groups ought to have some influence on the school board. But however chosen and however well intentioned and educated, the members of a single school board in a large city cannot possibly be informed about and interested in the school of each neighborhood, with its own ethnic, racial, and cultural peculiarities.

On the other hand, Katzman points out that, paradoxically, a large city school system, such as Boston's, affords lower class groups greater educational opportunities than do many small towns.[1] The low income districts of Boston receive a greater per pupil expenditure and have more highly competent staffs than do the school districts of small towns of comparable or higher income. Katzman also indicates that the higher income areas of Boston receive less expenditure per child than do the small towns of equal income. Although Katzman's information may be correct, there is little indication of local community involvement in Boston schools or of an over-all plan to deal with the urban school crisis at the grass roots level.

Another example of such attempts is found in New York. Italian was mostly taught in the high schools of Italian immigrant neighborhoods and Hebrew in those of Jewish neighborhoods many years ago, although these were not standard subjects in American high schools. However, Leonard Covello, in his book *The Heart Is the Teacher*, pointed out that a student in New York City could study Italian only after completing a year of Latin, French, or Spanish. It took a great deal of effort on the part of the Italian community to persuade the New York Board of Education to place Italian on an equal footing with other languages. In the 1930's Benjamin Franklin High School was built in East Harlem to serve the needs of that Italian neighborhood, and Covello, an Italian-American, was named its first principal.

Jews, in New York at least, have been relatively successful in gaining accommodation to their needs from the school system. Schools are closed on the Jewish holidays as well as at Christmas and Easter. In the schoolroom, some attention is given to the celebration of Hanukkah as well as to the singing of Christmas carols. German immigrants have always managed to have German taught in their schools, whether they settled in small towns or in big city neighborhoods. In northern Minnesota and northern Michigan, Scandianavian immigrants have been able to obtain curricular concessions to their languages and culture from the local schools. Although the needs of Mexican-Americans are often ignored in the elementary and high schools of Texas and New Mexico, it is no accident that both the University of New Mexico and the University of Texas have developed excellent programs in Spanish language and literature as well as in Latin American culture.

Other groups have also been successful in obtaining accommodation from the schools. In Polish and Slovak neighborhoods of large cities, attention is given to the customs and holidays of Poland and Slovakia. The band at a dance at a high school in a Polish neighborhood may well play mostly polkas. In Hungarian neighborhoods, the girls may attend high school dances in costume. Often the teachers have the same national origin as do the parents of the neighborhood and can tell and understand a joke in Polish, Slovak, or Hungarian, as the case may be. When the public schools cannot or will not make such accommodations, parochial schools are sometimes founded which provide cultural identity as well as religious instruction. Thus, Chicago has Irish Catholic schools, Polish Catholic schools, Slovak Catholic schools, and even Slovak Lutheran schools, as alternatives to the public school system.

In many places where school boards have tried to make some accommodation to the needs of minority groups, these attempts have been sporadic and each new accommodation has required additional effort on the part of the affected community. But the school boards of many cities are not so responsive to the needs of particular minorities as was the New York City Board of Education to the needs of the New York Italian and Jewish communities, for example. Most important, such accommodations as are made come in the form of largess from the upper middle class school board and are usually the result of political maneuvering or logrolling among various minority groups. In one of the examples above, the members of the East Harlem Italian community were not given any authority or control even over the high school that was called theirs.

Other minorities do not fare as well, even in New York. The Negro, Puerto Rican, and Mexican-American minorities in most of our cities were not even heard by the school board in the past. Even the white poor have had little or no influence.

The middle class members of the urban community have had an advantage in their contacts with boards of education, the superintendent's office, the principal's office, or other agencies. The children of parents of means have had a special voice, have always received special consideration, and have seemed to have a special key which opened many doors. Their parents received exceptional treatment from the principal and the teachers when they came to the school. The teachers often recognized them as civic leaders. These parents were not ignorant. They were able to communicate. They dressed in a middle or upper class fashion. Their articulation was often superior to that of the teacher, their income larger than that of the teacher, and their influence with the school administration greater than that of the teacher. Above all, the middle and upper class parents were not afraid to come to the school, as lower class parents so often are. It is the children of such parents as these who receive the special treatment and consideration.

Research studies contain ample evidence that the public in most communities have been run by and for the more privileged groups of society. For example, August de B. Hollingshead, in his classic study *Elmtown's Youth* ("Elmtown" is a small midwestern city), found that the board of education felt responsible only to the upper and middle classes in discharging its professional responsibilities. The members of the board of education did not conceive of the education of the lower classes as part of their responsibility. Furthermore, the lower classes were not represented on the board. It was even alleged by Hollingshead that an influential citizen of the community could bring pressure to bear on the school system to raise the grades of his child, so that the child could enter the college of his choice. Obviously, the child of a member of a lower class must be satisfied with the grades assigned him by his teachers. Many Elmtown teachers were found to grade students with an eye to the status of the parent, as a means of assuring their own advancement. Even the enforcement of rules in the schools was limited by the influence of the upper classes in the community.

Another example is the study by W. Lloyd Warner entitled *Democracy in Jonesville* ("Jonesville" is a corn-belt city), which revealed that the better grades went to the students of higher social class and the poorer grades to the students of lower social class. Of course, it may well be that the children of parents higher on the social scale performed better, on an objective basis, for a variety of reasons, but Warner carefully indicated that behind these figures lies an intricate patter of interaction, motives, and desires among the various classes. Teachers in Jonesville soon learned "who is who" and what must be done to satisfy the people who count in the community. Experienced teachers oriented the new teachers regarding the social-class background of each student. In subtle ways the teachers of Jonesville learned to act judiciously in their relations with students of varing social-class backgrounds. There is little doubt that the teachers of Jonesville, like the teachers of Elmtown and a host of other cities and towns in this country, catered to the children of the prominent families of the community and especially to the children of school board members.

Further studies can be cited to substantiate the obvious conclusion of the illustrations given above. Among these are *Plainville, Vansburg, Northeast City, Georgia Town, Prairietown, Yankee City, Deep South, Middletown,* and *Middletown in Transition.*

The poor can no longer be ignored in school planning and in the formulation of policy. In the past, middle class city school boards have given considerable evidence of their inability even to understand the problems and aspirations of the urban poor and the ethnic and racial minorities who live in city ghettos. As the exodus of the middle class from the city, described in Chapter I, continues, schools will have to rely more and more on the resources of those left behind.

The poor and the various ethnic and racial minorities in our cities usually live in well-defined neighborhoods, separated from the declining number of middle class neighborhoods and from one another as well. The inhabitants of a city neighborhood should have substantial autonomy in the operation of their own schools. The school-community partnership can be strengthened and a greater understanding of school problems be developed only through authentic communication and involvement on the part of the neighborhood residents. The middle class suburbanite would not tolerate a school system run by some agency external to his suburb. Neither would he permit an educational experiment to be conducted in his child's school by an outside agency without prior consultation with him or his neighbors or the local parent association.

The Adams-Morgan Community School Project which was carried out in Washington, D.C., as a joint venture sponsored by the Antioch-Putnam Graduate School of Education, the Washington, D.C., public schools, and the Morgan School Community is an example of such an experiment.

Paul Lauter, who directed this project, has described the difficulties encountered.[2] In the first place, the project was the result of consultation between representatives of the college and the school superintendent. Only after the initial plans were made was there consultation with the community leadership. When the project began, it was found that the project staff was completely unable to deal with the divergent demands of the Negro and white parents. Lauter reports that white parents wanted French taught, but that Negro parents, for the most part, considered French an unnecessary frill. White parents were willing to accept some course work in Negro history, but were opposed to the degree of emphasis on black culture and the number of Negro teachers that Negro parents wished. Although white students represented only 3 percent of the student population, the whites were able to elect half of this neighborhood's representatives to the school board, which would seem to indicate black alienation from schools, even almost entirely black schools. The whole project ended with the parents of both groups displaying considerable hostility to the project staff, and almost nothing was accomplished.

We propose that the concept of the neighborhood school district with its own elected school board be established in our largest cities. In some cases there would be a problem in drawing lines between adjacent neighborhoods, but such problems would not be more severe than the problem of dividing one district into attendance areas, which is now solved in one way or another. The dividing lines may seem quite arbitrary to some, but so do the lines that divide one suburb from another or from the central city in certain instances.

A school board that is elected by a neighborhood might be expected to have the same ethnic, racial, and economic characteristics as the neighborhood. Small towns do not ordinarily elect school boards that represent the poor and ethnic and racial minorities, as Hollingshead and others have pointed out. However, a neighborhood of a large city can be expected to have a more homogeneous population than do many small towns. It is true that, particularly near the core of the city, pockets of luxury will often be found in neighborhoods mostly inhabited by the poor, but such a spread will not exist in most neighborhoods. A small town may be divided into white and Negro, with the school board dominated by whites; but a city neighborhood may be all Negro (or all Puerto Rican, or all Mexican-American, or inhabited by poor whites), so that members of the underprivileged classes will of necessity become school board members. Economically deprived neighborhoods will elect representatives who are from the poor or at least live in the neighborhood, giving to the community its first official representation in the educational establishment.

The possibility of election to school board membership will give each neighborhood an opportunity to develop its own leadership, particularly in educational matters. In the opinion of the authors, such leadership will be responsive to the needs and aspirations of the residents of the neighborhood. One can question the advisability of giving the poor, usually relatively uneducated people, this important power and responsibility; on the other hand, these neighborhoods already elect their own representatives to the state legislature and even to Congress, Therefore, there is no valid reason why neighborhoods housing the poor or members of minorities should not be allowed to elect people like themselves to run their own schools. The middle class has always demanded this right, and now others are demanding it as well.

The neighborhood school board would be empowered to hire and fire both teachers and school administrators, subject only to the state certification requirements and tenure regulations. The neighborhood board could also establish, within the framework of state requirements, a curriculum to serve the particular interests and needs of the community. For example, a Negro neighborhood school might well offer some courses in Negro history and Swahili, just as a small rural town might offer course work in agriculture. The neighborhood residents would decide for themselves whether to emphasize the college preparatory or the vocational curriculum.

With the control of the school in neighborhood hands, the alienation of the poor and minority groups from the neighborhood school hopefully would be minimized. The parents, being now more involved with the school, might be expected to assist school authorities in the enforcement of school attendance laws. Also, once the neighborhood recognizes that school property is theirs, vandalism on school property is not likely to be tolerated by the community. Therefore, both truancy and vandalism can be expected to decrease.

The big city neighborhood school board would differ from the small town school board in that it would not have the usual fiscal responsibility. Poor sections of the city must have financial assistance for their schools from wealthier sections if the cycle of poverty is ever to be broken. Unfortunately, the middle class may prefer to isolate themselves from the poor, so that they can provide good schools for their children without having to support schools for the children of the needy. The suburbs offer them this opportunity. On the other hand, the greater degree of industrialization of the city may provide a sufficient tax base to provide for schools for the poor, even without middle class support. Ideally, the fiscal responsibility for the city's schools should be in the hands of a city-wide board. The city board would also make decisions concerning capital investment, as it does now.

There are numerous difficulties, however, among which is the fact that many professional educators are not happy with some aspects of school decentralization, as proposed in the Bundy Report. In particular, the United Federation of Teachers feels that job security is threatened. Also, the residents of some neighborhoods, not being informed in educational matters, may not understand or appreciate the concept of tenure. "After all," he may argue, "I do not have tenure in my job. If my superiors consider my work unsatisfactory, I can be discharged. Why should my school board not be empowered to fire a teacher or principal if I and my neighbors consider him unsatisfactory?" Naturally, any denial of the concept of tenure tends to alarm teachers and their professional organizations. On the other hand, the school can and should be very important to the life of the neighborhood. Small towns and even middle class neighborhoods have found means to eliminate teachers they considered undesirable, by either dismissal or transfer. Over a period of years, middle class citizens have been able to influence hiring policies to the point that dissatisfaction with either a teacher or a principal is less likely to develop. Most problems of this type, although serious, would probably be temporary after the transition to the new pattern was completed.

However, the seriousness of problems during the transition

has been brought before the public very forcefully by the situation surrounding the lengthy New York City teachers' strike during the fall of 1968. No one can propose decentralization without taking cognizance of the circumstances surrounding New York's attempts at decentralization and the resulting problems.

In May, 1968, ten teachers in the Ocean Hill-Brownsville District of Brooklyn were dismissed from their positions by the neighborhood board for allegedly attempting to sabotage school decentralization or for other reasons. Other teachers left their posts in sympathy. Although the ten teachers were cleared of the charges against them and although the City Board branded their dismissal as illegal, the neighborhood governing board refused to reinstate them the following September. The United Federation of Teachers called a strike on the opening day of school, in protest.

Two days later, the strike was settled by a promise of reinstatement to the dismissed teachers. However, residents of the neighborhood barred their entry into the school. As a result, the United Federation of Teachers called another strike, because of the failure of the New York City Board of Education to enforce the settlement. Dr. James E. Allen, then State Commissioner of Education, was asked to intervene, and on September 14 he ordered the City Board to suspend the neighborhood board and to transfer the ten teachers temporarily. The City Board followed orders, but the teachers voted to continue the strike. The teachers complained of harassment and even of threats to their safety and demanded protection. They persuaded the City Board to order reinstatement of the teachers who had supported the originally dismissed ten teachers, but the neighborhood unit administrator, Rhody A. McCoy, refused to do so.

Schools were ordered to reopen on September 30. Both the neighborhood board and the ten teachers were reinstated. But on October 1, a battle between supporters of the neighborhood school board and the police took place. The neighborhood board was suspended for thirty days, and McCoy was removed from his post for refusing to assign the ten teachers to classroom duties. On October 14, the teachers again voted to strike, charging that their lives had been threatened.

Mayor Lindsay was in communication with both sides of the

dispute and appointed a panel to settle it. Both sides refused to submit to binding arbitration. Governor Nelson Rockefeller expressed his concern and considered calling a special session of the state legislature to deal with the crisis. The strike was finally settled on November 18, and the teachers returned to their duties on November 19, 1968. However, disagreeable confrontations and uproar have continued.

Most observers, including State Senate majority leader Earl W. Brydges, feel that the legislature will move much more slowly on decentralization than seemed probable earlier in the year. It seems likely that stronger legislation outlawing strikes by teachers will be passed, in spite of vigorous objections by the United Federation of Teachers. On the other hand, other legislation will probably give stronger protection to teachers' rights. But whatever happens, minority groups in New York will continue to demand more local control of schools and will, in time, see some of their demands met.

Within the existing framework, the recruitment of ghetto teachers has been a serious problem. Some beginning teachers have been willing to teach in a ghetto school, but usually when enough seniority is gained to enable them to transfer to a school in a middle or upper class neighborhood they do so. Teacher turnover is far greater in ghetto schools than in other neighborhood schools, and, as was pointed out in Chapter I, the use of substitute teachers is much greater in ghetto schools. It cannot be pretended that the creation of neighborhood school boards will eliminate this problem. Local boards will have to make concerted efforts to retain experienced teachers, as well as to recruit other teachers, both white and black.

We have discussed the idea of neighborhood control of schools in contradistinction to city or state control. Another possibility, although not broached very often or very seriously, is the idea of a national or federal school system, such as is common in other countries. Paradoxically, there seems reason to believe that federal control would benefit the schools of ghetto neighborhoods. Federal involvement may well come if local governments do not succeed in solving their school problems, just as it has come in other areas after local and state governments have failed to act.

The federal government could establish a uniform curriculum

for each level, allowing some minor variations to fit local needs. Students could be given nationally standardized examinations so that the quality of education in one part of the country could be compared with that in another at every educational level. National certification requirements for teachers and principals could be imposed, allowing teachers to move freely from one state to another. Perhaps some married female teachers who follow their husbands' jobs across state lines would not be lost to the profession. Also, there would be no loss of pension credit or service time to the teacher who sought to teach in another state.

The federal government could establish a uniform per pupil expenditure, taking into account differing costs in different parts of the country, so that a child would have the same educational opportunity whether he lived in Mississippi, New York, or California and whether he lived in a village, a middle class suburb, or an urban ghetto. A national salary scale for teachers would be possible, again taking regional costs of living into account.

Probably both the urban poor and the suburban middle class would oppose such a national educational program. But, in time, the poor and the members of minority groups may recall that they have always had a fairer deal from the federal government than from most state and local governments. Federal poverty programs came into being because of the unwillingness or the inability of state and local governments to deal with the problems of poverty. Federal public accommodations laws and fair employment acts came into being because state and local governments had failed to act. In very many areas—including minimum wage laws, treatment of minorities in government employment and in the Armed Forces, and the Supreme Court decisions affecting school integration—the federal government has shown itself more sympathetic with the problems of the poor and deprived minorities than have other levels of government.

Although not within the scope of this book, it might be mentioned that many of our largest cities have had to turn to the federal government for assistance with a variety of problems, in large measure because their state legislatures, dominated by rural interest, had turned a deaf ear to their pleas for assistance. Federal urban housing, federally financed city freeways, and federal aid to schools and hospitals are all examples of the failures of state and local governments.

A federally controlled national school system is not being proposed here, although such a system would offer some advantages. What Americans have always wanted is local control of their schools. The tragedy is that a large segment of our population has never enjoyed this privilege. The urban poor and deprived groups are now demanding the same right that the middle class groups have always enjoyed. If their demands are ignored, it seems clear that they will turn to the federal government for assistance with this problem, as they have in the past with other problems. It is well to remember that our nation is becoming increasingly urbanized, that the House of Representatives of our Congress is relatively fairly apportioned as regards population, and that not even Presidential candidates are able to ignore the wishes and desires of poor and minority groups.

It should be clear that the chief cause of the difficulties in establishing neighborhood control of schools, which have been described, is the lack of planning and communication. Guidelines must be carefully drawn that delineate the authority of the neighborhood board and the limitations of its authority. These guidelines must be made known to the community at large. We can no longer permit plans to initiate school decentralization to be hastily drawn, whether by school boards, legislatures, or private foundations. Without careful planning and communication among all affected levels and agencies, teachers' strikes, ugly racial confrontations, and general confusion may result. The poor want and have a right to be heard. They are going to have schools more to their liking, one way or another.

NOTES

[1]Martin T. Katzman, "Decentralizing the Big City Schools," *Urban Education*, III (1968), 156–159.
[2]Paul Lauter, "The Short, Happy Life of the Adams-Morgan Community School Project," *Harvard Educational Review*, XXXVIII (Spring, 1968), 257–258.

CHAPTER V

Higher Education Faces the Urban Challenge

The great universities of the European Continent were and are clearly associated with great European cities. The universities of Paris, Vienna, Berlin, Rome, and Madrid are natural and obvious examples. The faculties of such universities live in the city, and the students, whether or not they come from the city, often take an active part in the political, social, and cultural life of the city. The massive student demonstrations at the University of Paris and at the University of Madrid during 1968 clearly indicate the involvement of those student bodies with national affairs.

The traditional concept of university education in the United States is very different, although the recent student demonstrations at Columbia University and on other campuses indicate a countertrend. With the exception of a few private universities, which are often ideologically remote from the cities in which they are located, the American concept has been to associate a university or college with a small "college town."

As an ever growing majority of American youth are being educated in publicly supported as opposed to privately supported institutions, it might be appropriate to examine the state universities that have in the past been phenomena of the South and Middle West and more recently of the West. State universities, with only a few exceptions such as the University of Minnesota, the University of Washington, and the University of California at Los Angeles, were originally located in small towns, while the largest city in a state was ignored as far as a state university was concerned. State teachers colleges or normal schools were also located in small towns and rural areas and trained rural youth to become teachers in rural schools, even if they eventually taught in cities.

In some cases the rural-dominated state legislature feared that the youth would be contaminated by contact with the supposed evils of a large city. More than a hundred years ago the Louisiana legislature considered and rejected the idea of establishing Louisiana State University in New Orleans. Instead, the state university was located in Baton Rouge, which was then a very small city, in order to protect Louisiana youth from the "sin" that was supposedly so prevalent in New Orleans. In many cases agriculture was an important part of the curriculum, so that a rural location was essential. Until World War II, and in many cases even later, such states as Pennsylvania, Massachusetts, New Jersey, North Carolina, Virginia, Louisiana, Texas, Indiana, Illinois, Kansas, and Ohio did not provide state-supported universities in their largest cities. Furthermore, New York State did not even have a state university.

With the end of World War II and the flood of veterans demanding that higher education be made available to them by the GI Bill of Rights, most states made some effort to provide higher education in urban communities, at least in the form of extension centers. Later the idea of a major state university campus in each large city came into being. We now have the Chicago Circle Campus of the University of Illinois, the University of Missouri at St. Louis and at Kansas City, the University of Wisconsin at Milwaukee, Louisiana State University at New Orleans, and many others. The extension of campuses of the University of California is one of the fantastic accomplishments of our age. In addition, states began to take over private or municipal universities already located in large cities. The Municipal University of Wichita became Wichita State University, the University of Buffalo became the State University of New York at Buffalo, and the University of Chattanooga passed under state control, renamed the University of Tennessee at Chattanooga, to mention only a few. Later, Indiana began to make the urban two-year extension centers of Indiana University into four-year institutions.

When a state legislature has decided to locate a state university campus in a given city, the problem of location is not solved. Should the campus be located in one of the city's ghettos, where land can be obtained through urban renewal? The ghetto location would encourage ghetto residents to attend and would eliminate problems of transportation for them. Also, such a campus might well provide cultural opportunity for even the nonstudent residents of the area. The City University of New York has recently located a new campus in Jamaica in the heart of a Negro community. On the other hand, some critics of this move contend that it cannot be expected that middle class youth, in large numbers, will come to a ghetto-located campus, so that the slum student would be deprived of association with students from other social backgrounds.

Another concept is to locate the urban campus in a fringe area, between a ghetto and another type of area. The location of the Chicago Circle Campus of the University of Illinois is an example. Presumably, such a campus location would produce a more diversified student body, especially in a publicly supported commuter institution.

Strange to say, some urban campuses are located in a section of a city where every resident sends his son or daughter to an out-of-town institution. The New Orleans campus of Louisiana State University is located adjacent to homes costing in excess of $100,000 and miles from the worst Negro ghetto sections. Even more absurd is the location of at least one so-called urban campus at a site several miles outside the metropolitan area. On the other hand, the University of Tennessee at Chattanooga is located in the heart of Chattanooga.

Whenever a campus of the major state university is located in a city, the urban campus remains subordinate to the old campus. Sometimes a completely new urban university is founded, such as Cleveland State University in Ohio. But even a new urban state university usually lacks both the prestige and the funding of the older state university. As an example, for the academic year 1967–1968 the average faculty salary at Cleveland State University was $10,534, as compared with $12,728 for the same year at Ohio State University.[1] Such salary differentials exist between the older state university and the new urban universities of other states, as well. There is even a substantial faculty salary differential between urban and rural campuses of the same state university, in spite of the fact that the living and commuting costs for the urban university professor may be higher. For example, in 1967–1968 the average faculty salary at the New Orleans campus of Louisiana State University was $9,644, as compared with $11,580 at the parent campus in Baton Rouge.[2] The important political figures in the state are likely to be alumni of the more established university, who back up their institutional loyalty with meaningful support. The older campus has the staff, buildings, research centers, graduate programs, and reputation to attract better faculty and students. The faculty and administration, as well as the alumni, of the established university have a vested interest in maintaining their institution's pre-eminent position.

Still, the urban university attracts students, particularly students of low economic status. Such students can find attendance at even an urban, publicly supported institution expensive. With the exception of the City University of New York and a few other urban universities, tuition can be high, up to several hundred dollars per semester. Again with only a few exceptions, transportation can be a problem, as many cities do not have adequate public transportation, and students must own automobiles out of necessity. Books, laboratory fees, and incidentals add to the cost of education. On the bright side, the urban location usually provides decent employment opportunities, as compared with those available in the small college town, where the college student and his wife have so often been exploited.

The urban and particularly the ghetto student may have low academic potential, as measured either by high school grades or by standardized tests. If the urban campus of the state university imposes the same entrance standards as at its established campus, such students will not be admitted. On the other hand, if entrance requirements are reduced for some students, there is no guarantee that these students will achieve academic success. It is interesting to note that the entrance requirements of the City University of New York have generally exceeded those of the State University Colleges of New York, so that the City University has existed primarily for the intellectual and academic elite. Many New York City youth were denied opportunity for higher education, not by financial status, since the City University charges no tuition, but by failing to be academically superior.

Recently, the City University has relaxed its entrance requirements somewhat, particularly for students identified as "culturally deprived." It is too soon to say whether students admitted
under the relaxed standards will be able to benefit from exposure
to an academic program which was designed for superior students. But this relaxation of entrance requirements for certain
students was one of the objections raised by middle class parents
in the "middle class revolt" mentioned in Chapter I. However, it
is hoped that students admitted to the City University will receive
adequate tutorial assistance and guidance.

The urban university has a special obligation to assist underprivileged youth. Merely to relax entrance requirements and
place young people in a curricular situation in which failure is
almost certain is not the answer. Disadvantaged youth will need
special guidance and counseling and probably the addition of
remedial courses to the curriculum. Most urban high schools provide commercial or "shop" programs as alternatives to the standard college preparatory curriculum. Students who have completed one of these so-called terminal high school programs will
need to make up some deficiencies. They will need help in understanding the tremendous variety of courses available. Above all,
they will need special instruction in the use of the library, in use
of study time, and in how to take notes in the large lecture classes
which are becoming the standard mode of instruction in freshman courses.

Many such students experience great difficulty in reading and
in mathematics. Reading is clearly an essential skill for all academic work. Poor readers can easily be detected by testing and
can be assigned to reading clinics. Deficiencies in mathematics
limit the educational and occupational goals of the students. Remedial courses and extensive tutorial programs are needed in
this area. If the urban campus has a graduate program, graduate
students can be given employment as tutors to students deficient
in background.

The community college has come into being partly to provide
higher educational opportunity for the less gifted student. The
community college normally operates an "open door" admission policy to a much greater extent than does any senior college

or university. In order that the open door policy does not become a "revolving door" policy, by which many students are forced to withdraw for academic reasons within a semester or so after admission, students are given more and better counseling than in many universities. Remedial work—that is, high school course work—is usually offered, without apology. Often, potentially good students can be "saved" within the college parallel program of a community college. The student with deficiencies may correct them. He may learn good study habits and improve his reading and computational skills. With these tools in hand, he will have an opportunity to move toward a degree, at either the urban or rural state university campus.

The growth of community colleges is often deplored by university faculty and administrators. Yet, it is the failure of the university, even the urban university, to provide the kinds of assistance described above which has contributed to the establishment of so many community colleges. If our universities had been willing to accept the challenge posed by the disadvantaged student, much of the support which now goes to community colleges might have been given to the universities.

Community colleges usually offer training in vocational and technical subjects as well as typical college courses. Such programs may be derided by university professors, but there is a demand for such training, both on the part of students and on the part of prospective employers. A case might be made for separating college parallel community colleges from technical and vocational ones, but in many areas such a separation would not be economically feasible. And one of the advantages of the combination is that a student is enabled to change his educational goals within the same institution. In any case, most universities offer nothing to take the place of the vocational training available in many community colleges.

Community college vocational training may be regarded as terminal, but the student in the college parallel program will normally expect that some college or university will give transfer credit for his community college work. It is fashionable for the faculties of senior institutions to question the quality of courses being transferred from a community college. However, the difficulties encountered by the transfer student are much more serious in disciplines which have a vertical, sequential structure. Particular examples are mathematics and foreign languages. Whether transfer credit is allowed or not, the transfer student must expect to be able to enroll in the next course in the sequence after he has transferred. Thus, he has a right to demand that his previous courses in the community college have adequately prepared him for the course work ahead of him. But it is often the case that the student transferring from the community college finds himself at a serious disadvantage in the disciplines previously mentioned.

The very phrase "college parallel" raises the natural question, "parallel to what?" With a lack of experience on the part of both the community college faculty and administration with college courses, how can they tell that the courses which they offer are the proper sort for freshmen and sophomores in college to be taking? However, we are not here raising the question of the training and quality of the community college faculty.[3] Even if the community college faculty is no less well qualified than that portion of the faculty of a four-year college or university which teaches freshmen and sophomore courses, it must be remembered that the senior college and the university have senior faculty members who are available to devise the curriculum even at the freshman and sophomore levels and to advise the junior faculty on appropriate educational matters. But usually the community college faculty member has no one to whom he can turn.[4]

The urban university student differs from other university students in other ways than in his economic and academic situation. Being from the same city, he and his fellow students will be very much alike in tastes, interests, and their understandings of the world at large. He is almost certain to be employed and is even likely to be employed full time. He may well place the demands of his job higher on his scale of priorities than the demands of his studies, so that he differs from the typical working student at a rural campus. The urban university schedules many of its courses in the evening, to accommodate his working schedule.

He is not so likely to identify closely with his university campus. While it is true that some urban universities now have dormitories, these typically accommodate only a small fraction of the student body, so that the urban university student is likely to continue to live in the same neighborhood in which he grew up. He is, therefore, likely to look to his neighborhood for his entertainment and recreation rather than to his university. Consequently, he is less interested in intercollegiate athletics, fraternities and sororities, dances and social functions, and even the concerts, lectures, films, and other cultural opportunities provided by the university, than is his rural counterpart. In fact, the urban university is likely to disrupt its classes in order to schedule lectures or cultural programs during prime class time, such as 10:00 A.M., whereas a rural campus would offer such programs in the late afternoon so as to offer minimal interference with classes. The urban university student has left the campus for his own neighborhood by late afternoon and is not likely to return in order to attend a lecture or concert.

Although deplored by many educators, the fact is that the urban university student, like the urban university professor, in many cases, comes to the campus for his classes and then goes home. At many urban campuses, faculty office space is so limited that a faculty member must share an office with several other faculty members. He may find it difficult to do his work under such conditions, so there is little reason for him to remain on the campus after teaching his classes and holding his office hours.

There are urban universities which do succeed in recruiting some students from rural areas. Also, many of them have been able to attract a fair number of foreign students, who may prefer urban to rural living. The foreign student may expect to find a fair number of his fellow countrymen or American citizens of his national origin in a large city. Sometimes he will find an association or club formed by people from his own country, and he can usually find a Cosmopolitan Club. When graduate programs are established, it will be the case that the graduate student body is considerably more cosmopolitan than the undergraduate student body, and citizens of foreign countries are more likely to be graduate than undergraduate students. But, for the most part, urban university student bodies, particularly the undergraduates, are quite local, especially in tax-supported institutions.

To some extent, American universities, whether urban or

rural, have failed to recognize the fact that the typical American university student body has changed. The liberal and classical traditions which have formed the foundations of higher education and are still praised so highly by important educators, such as Robert Hutchins and Mark Van Doren, do not seem relevant to today's student. Although we may regret it, the fact is that the young person expects higher education to train him for some profession or occupation. We have all been told how many more thousands of dollars the college-educated person can expect to earn, as compared with the high school graduate. Is it any wonder that our students have believed it?

A great controversy now surrounds the purposes and goals of the university. Many laymen, including well-educated laymen, view the university primarily as an institution that teaches young people. Traditionally, universities have seen themselves as performing the threefold purpose of preserving, transmitting, and increasing knowledge. James A. Perkins, President of Cornell University, has compared the modern university to a triangle having three equal sides representing teaching, research, and public service.[5] But the fact is that academic and financial rewards seem to go to the published researcher far more often than to the great teacher. In recent years we have seen professors, presumably great teachers and certainly well liked by their students, dismissed from their posts by reason of an inadequate publication record. Student demonstrations have occurred on more than one campus for this reason alone.

In the past the public service and research sides of the Perkins triangle were often intertwined. Faculty members sought and obtained research grants from various agencies of the federal government and often from various branches of the military. The universities encouraged their faculty to seek such grants, and many professors found it possible to redirect their interests into areas where support would be available. The award of a research grant to a faculty member has become such a status symbol that a professor on an urban campus once proposed that membership in the graduate faculty be limited to faculty members doing "sponsored research." The fact that research grants are more often available in some disciplines than in others was ignored by this faculty member.

Much of this sponsored research has been in support of what some call the "military-industrial complex." Militant students, already angered by the lack of interest in teaching on the part of their professors and even their absence from class while doing consulting work, found a new cause for complaint. Students who oppose American intervention in Vietnam found that some of their professors were aiding the military in the war effort, and sometimes expressed their outrage in demonstrations.

At the same time, professors in a variety of fields find themselves being consulted on all sorts of public questions. Universities as institutions are being asked to involve themselves with a host of questions that seem to some to be outside the academic purview. Professor Jacques Barzun, of Columbia University, has charged that universities are destroying themselves by rushing here and there to aid anyone in distress, as does the Red Cross.[6] Barzun seems to prefer that the university retain its ivory-tower image.

Dr. Clark Kerr, former President of the University of California and now head of the Commission on the Future of Higher Education, takes an opposing view.[7] He claims that universities have always offered service to society, but that in the past it was service to the status quo and the aristocracy. He sees the university as playing an important role in the solution of the most pressing domestic problems of our day, which are primarily urban problems. Dr. Kerr said in a recent speech, "It is a question whether universities should serve the people in the urban ghettos or the military-industrial complex, whether they want to serve criticism and dissent or the status quo."

Both Barzun and Kerr were talking about universities in general, but surely the problems of "people in the urban ghettos" must be of even greater concern to the urban universities than to those in rural locations. Many university administrators do not see the choice as Kerr does. And many of the University of California students who rioted while Kerr was president may not believe that Kerr is sincere in demanding that the university "serve criticism and dissent." Many students feel strongly that the standard academic approach is too remote and uninvolved to be relevant. Often they believe that their professors are too timid in opposing the evils of society or that they are profiting from them.

Professors who expect to obtain research grants from the various agencies of the defense department are under some pressure to avoid open criticism of American Vietnam policy, for example. Problems encountered by a group of mathematicians who have been frankly opposed to our Vietnam policy were well described in the Letters to the Editor section of all the 1968 issues of the *Notices* of the American Mathematical Society, and elsewhere. There is no way of knowing how many university professors have been silenced by a threat to their research contracts. But the danger is certainly there. Students are likely to admire neither timidity nor too active an interest in financial considerations on the part of their professors.

Urban universities have been founded in order to bring higher education to urban youth—the youth who might otherwise not obtain higher education. These young people are not wealthy; certainly not wealthy enough to engage in academic dilettantism. They want to be engineers, physicians, lawyers, teachers, and so on, rather than to be just educated. The fact that the students' occupational goals force them into required courses in humanities provides the professors of the humanities with a tremendous challenge, but such courses are not taught very differently to urban youth than they were to the sons of wealthy Virginia planters at William and Mary nearly three hundred years ago. Except that agriculture is not a part of the curriculum, the urban university curriculum differs very little from that of the rural university.

Of course, the urban university is in a sense self-contradictory. On one hand, the urban university should be concerned, in its research activities, with problems, whether medical, biological, chemical, political, or social, which are peculiarly urban and should provide something special in the way of education for its almost entirely urban-oriented student body. On the other hand, any university should concern itself to an extent with universal values and should take the urban student out of his home environment, at least intellectually. There is a need not only to explain his own culture and surroundings to the urban student but also to introduce him to the world at large. Some disciplines, such as mathematics, have no obvious urban-rural divisions, but others do.

Most urban universities are large enough to provide faculty members who have pure research interests as well as others with interests peculiar to urban areas. The biology and chemistry departments can surely afford one faculty member interested in the problem of urban pollution; the psychology department, a faculty member interested in industrial psychology; the sociology department, several faculty members interested in urban problems; the political science department, some faculty interested in municipal government; and so on. The urban location provides a ready-made laboratory for study in many areas.

A state university is usually controlled by a board of regents or trustees chosen so as to give representation to all geographic sections of the state. Such a board is almost certain not to represent the rural and urban sections of the state in proportion to the populations of these sections. In such cases, the board is dominated by rural interests. It is no surprise that such boards have not moved more quickly to establish urban universities. When such a university is founded, the rural board is not likely to consider urban experience or training an important qualification for its chief administrative officer. Therefore, an educator with no academic or personal experience with life in a large city may be appointed president or chancellor of the urban campus. He may even have all his degrees in an area very remote from urban concerns. When such an administrator assumes office, he may well appoint assistants and deans who, like himself, know little of city life and problems. The deans so chosen are unlikely to consider urban experience or training an important qualification when seeking to hire faculty. In fact, when a state university opens a branch campus in one of the state's urban centers, the administration and faculty of the branch campus are frequently drawn from the administration and faculty of the parent, rurally located campus. Sometimes it is charged that the parent campus uses the branch campus as a dumping ground for its undesirable personnel, who can be persuaded to move to the new campus in return for increase in rank or promotion to administrative responsibility. At an urban campus of one state university, 30 percent of the faculty received one or both of their advanced degrees from the parent, rurally located campus. It is not surprising that the parent campus feels superior to its urban branch when the hiring practices described above are so common.

The background of many of the trustees is felt not only in the hiring policies established for both administrative and teaching personnel but also in the rules laid down by the trustees for student conduct. The whole concept of *in loco parentis*, about which more will be said, is very different in an urban than in a rural setting, although urban campuses frequently have the same rules as do their parent rural campuses.

If a university is to be "universal," we might reasonably hope to expose our urban students to both rural-oriented and urban-oriented faculty. However, in some urban universities far too many of the faculty have lived all their lives and received all of their academic training, and maybe all of their academic experience, in a rural setting. Many such faculty do not even live in the city, but commute from the suburbs just like other middle class city employees. It is interesting to note that shortly after receiving a grant for the study of urban problems, Columbia University sought to purchase land in suburbia for the purpose of building a residential community in which to house its faculty. In many cases, then, the faculty and administration of the urban university are in, but not of, the city.

It should be mentioned here that some of the universities in New York City are an exception in this regard. Their problem is that almost all their faculty members are educational and sociological products of the city, with almost no experience outside of New York. The administration of the City University of New York has made great efforts to remedy this situation, but has not been very successful in attracting outsiders.

Physical facilities at urban universities are often inadequate, due in part to the greater cost of land and of construction in urban areas. The "campus setting" which is so important to the rural institution, with its trees, grass, shrubs, ponds, fountains, and quiet walkways, is often absent from the urban campus. In fact, it is only by courtesy that many urban universities can even be said to have a campus. If the campus center is considered so important to the rural environment, how much more important it is to the urban student, as well as to the city neighborhood in which the urban university happens to be located. Compared with the enormous Union Building or Campus Activity Center on a rural campus, the student lounges and the cafeterias of urban campuses seem dismal and very crowded. The absence of adequate eating and recreational facilities is alone sufficient to encourage the student to leave the urban campus when his classes are over. Although more important to the urban than to the rural student, the urban university library often offers much less in the way of study space and carrells.

The facilities for urban university faculty also compare unfavorably with those for rural university faculty members. There are few faculty lounges. Even faculty office space is at a premium, with many faculty members sharing the same office or even the same desk. The urban university often uses a large number of part-time faculty or lecturers, because these are available in urban centers and usually cost the university less than would additional faculty. These usually have no office space at all and are not available to students except in class.

The recent student riots and unrest have caused considerable consternation in adult circles. Students at all universities are beginning to resent the assumption of a parental role on the part of the university administration. Students also complain of the bigness and bureaucracy of the large university and of the dehumanization that bigness seems to cause. At every really large university, whether urban or rural, students find themselves reduced to identification numbers. They are compelled to stand in long lines to be registered by computing machines. They sit in enormous lecture rooms and listen to professors with whom they have no personal contact. But in spite of these similarities between the urban and rural universities, most of the dissatisfaction has been manifested by the urban student bodies.

It is often charged that the university is an ivory tower, remote from the real world. This charge is substantiated by both the admission policies and the curriculum. Tropman and Erlich have claimed that both university requirements and admission policies are simply statements of middle class values.[8] They further charge that the university protects and nurtures the middle class way of life, while insulating its students and faculty from other segments of society.

However, with both the student and the faculty member of an urban university living in areas remote from the classroom, the ivory-tower image is not so appropriate for the urban university. The student lives in his neighborhood, among people who work. He usually works himself. The issues of the day are found not only in his textbooks but in his life. Poverty and Vietnam, segregation and cultural deprivation, and unemployment are all real to him.

The student sees within his university the ever increasing specialization of our age. The university is organized into departments and subdepartments, and each faculty member has his own special field of interest, which is sometimes a niche rather than a branch of his discipline. In the world of work, however, the urban student can see the demand for persons more broadly trained and the co-operation, in the form of research teams, among persons expert in diverse disciplines. His concern about the value of the education he is receiving is understandable. When the student is denied meaningful articulation with the administration of his university, which often takes the parental attitude, "Daddy knows best," his reaction can be extreme. The unrest at Columbia came only after the administration refused to meet with student leaders to discuss issues of importance to the students. However, it must be recognized that a small segment of the student body seemed to want a militant confrontation on almost any issue.

Universities have dealt with student demands for a voice in their own destinies in diverse ways. Typically it is proposed that students be given representation on certain faculty committees. University administrations are quite often willing to have their faculties share some faculty prerogatives with students, but few administrative prerogatives have been granted to students. As the students generally make up a minority of any committee on which they serve, the faculty committee members can usually expect to outvote them. Perhaps some students are satisfied with an opportunity to be heard, but others are not. Also, at some campuses the students are not even allowed to control their student newspaper, yearbook, or radio station, even when the costs of these are paid wholly by the student in the form of fees or special assessments. As a general rule, students do not really expect their advice to be taken in all or even in very many cases, although there are exceptions. Violence on a campus erupts, not when student advice is not followed, but when the university officialdom refuses even to hear it.

Up to now the publicly supported urban university has been discussed, but most large cities contain one or more private colleges or universities. Usually the urban poor are denied admission to such institutions because of their relatively high tuition, and sometimes for academic or other reasons, as well. The more prestigious of these universities draw students on a national basis, so that their urban location may be irrelevant to their operations. On the other hand, there are many who now ask why any institution of higher learning should ignore its immediate environment.

Some urban private universities, of course, provide educational opportunity for the poor as their chief goal. Northeastern University in Boston operates a co-operative program which enables a student to alternate work and study in eight-week periods. Not only is a student able to support himself, but he can gain valuable experience related to his field of study at the same time. Other examples could be given, but it is difficult to avoid the conclusion that Catholic urban colleges and universities, like their Protestant counterparts, have not made a concerted effort to aid the central city poor.

A welcome countertrend is evident, however, in that there is an awakening on the part of some of these institutions to this problem and a commitment to the urban community in general. For example, Fordham University is planning specialized programs related to urban life and problems. A new pattern for the preparation of teachers is already under way. The School of

Social Service, under its new dean, James R. Dumpson, former Commissioner of Welfare in New York City, has added new dimensions to the training of social workers for the city. The Reverend Leo McLaughlin, S.J., Chancellor and former President of Fordham University, recently stated that his institution's location imposes "a strict obligation to serve the City at a time when people wonder if the City can survive."[9]

Yet, what has been cited is a relatively small accomplishment when contrasted with the many, and so far unsolved, problems. Almost every large metropolitan area has within its boundaries a large number of Catholic colleges and universities. The City of New Orleans supports three Catholic institutions of higher learning, all within its city limits. The City of Chicago and its suburbs currently include six Catholic institutions of higher learning, and New York has eight such institutions. But they have not focused their resources on the very people who now inhabit the city. On the other hand, these institutions with their limited financial resources cannot afford to provide expanded services within the present framework. The United States Office of Education recently reported that there were only nine Catholic institutions of higher learning in the United States (among the more than three hundred such institutions) with endowments of five million dollars or more. If Catholic institutions are going to meet the urban challenge, they will have to consolidate their resources as well as review their priorities during the coming decade. Also, greater effort will have to be made to recruit students from the ghettos. These students will need financial assistance if they are going to be able to attend college on a full-time basis. The time has come for private and church-supported colleges and universities to make a special effort to assist the poor.[10]

Urban universities have many problems. Like other universities, they are faced with ever mounting enrollments due to the high post–World War II birth rate and to the increased demand for higher education. Like other universities, they need more and better facilities. The special problems of urban universities are being attacked, but the attack must be speeded up. Students with nonacademically oriented backgrounds must be attracted. Faculty members attuned to urban problems must be recruited.

But, above all, the urban university must take cognizance of its urban setting and not simply be a rural university that happens to be located in a city.

NOTES

[1]"Annual Report of the Economic Status of the Professor, 1967–1968," *AAUP Bulletin* 54, (June, 1968), p. 228.

[2]*Ibid.*, p. 217.

[3]See Philip D. Vairo, "Faculty Quality: A Challenge for the Community College," *Journal of Higher Education,* XXXVI (April, 1965), 217–220, for additional comment.

[4]See William M. Perel and Philip D. Vairo, "The Community College and the College Parallel Program," *Journal of Higher Education*, XL (January, 1969), 47–52, for additional comment. Copyright © 1969 by the Ohio State University Press and reprinted with its permission.

[5]New York *Times,* Education Section, November 3, 1968, p. 11.

[6]New York *Times,* October 31, 1968, p. 20.

[7]*Ibid.*

[8]John E. Tropman and John L. Erlich, "New Political Realities: Academia and the City," *Journal of Higher Education,* XXXIX (June, 1968), 303.

[9]*Report of the President,* Fordham University, 1965–1967, p. 7.

[10]See William M. Perel and Philip D. Vairo, "The Catholic University and College—Today and Tomorrow," *Liberal Education,* LIV (December, 1968), 528–532, for additional comment.

CHAPTER VI

The Urban Community Views Its Schools and Colleges

As the United States developed, small towns grew into cities as a result of immigration, both from rural areas and from foreign countries. Foreign immigrants came to find opportunity, including educational opportunity, which was denied to them in their native lands.

Harry Golden, in his newspaper the *Carolina Israelite*, has written much about the eastern European Jewish immigrants in New York. Some of these immigrants already had some education, but even the majority who had little education respected it and demanded it for their children. The better-educated among them founded schools in which they taught their fellow immigrants. These one-teacher, back-room schools often had a two-subject curriculum, English and Hebrew. The need for English as a means to further occupational goals and cultural accommodation on a foreign shore is readily understandable. But the study of Hebrew was intended for a quite different purpose.

While the Hebrew language has considerable religious significance for Jewish people, it also has cultural implications. If English were studied with the idea of assimilation in mind, Hebrew was studied, at least partly, to maintain cultural identity. No one claimed that the study of Hebrew was relevant to employment. Neither was it demanded as a prerequisite to higher education. But Jewish parents wanted to learn and wanted their children to learn who they were.

Jewish children attended public schools run by and for the older immigrants, who were steeped in Christian culture. The school children sang Christmas carols around a school Christmas tree, but the Jewish children persistently maintained their identity. The Irish and Italian immigrants had their problems of assimilation, but they too, in different ways, maintained their own identities. The Irish and Italian people were denied admission to some of the existing institutions of higher learning, by quota systems and other discriminatory admission policies. They usually attended Catholic institutions or local tax-supported institutions, if available. Later, Irish and Italian young people moved on to the more cosmopolitan universities. Somehow, the older immigrant groups became culturally and economically assimilated to some extent without losing many of the aspects of culture that set them apart.

Today, our cities face a new kind of immigration. The Negro, the Puerto Rican, and the rural poor white are all coming to the city to find greater opportunity, just as did the foreign immigrants. But the new immigrants differ markedly from the old. Harry Golden's efforts to identify the emergence of the Negro and his migration to the city with the immigration of eastern European Jews to New York are interesting and entertaining, but have little relation to reality. In an address delivered at the University of North Carolina at Charlotte in 1966, he claimed that the Jewish immigrants were successful in achieving economic and even literary success because they tried harder, or, in his words, "not because they were better, but because they did not think they were as good." He described the Jew's demand for education as a means of achieving status with the statement, "He knew that if he had a stethoscope around his neck, people would no longer consider him alien, but would only say, 'My doctor has such a cute accent!' "

There is in the background of the Negro a record of slavery, segregation, exploitation, and barbarous cruelty dating back several hundred years, at least, and unrelieved by even a brief period of ascendancy. The Negro has had no reason to value education, since he has had little opportunity for education in the past and has been discriminated against by the very institution which has purported to help him. More important, Negroes who did succeed in obtaining education were not accorded the status to which education would have entitled a white person. The

Negro who received an M.D. degree was not even called "doctor" by some whites. He had to live in segregated housing and send his children to segregated schools. In some instances, he was not even allowed entry into the only hospital in his town.

There is no solution for the problem of assimilation for the Negro. Wherever he goes and whatever he does, he takes with him his black skin. Learning English, becoming educated, and even making a great deal of money in our money-conscious society are not enough for the Negro, as they have been for Jewish, Irish, and Italian immigrants. But the Negro finds it difficult to achieve even that which is possible. In the South he is the product of segregated and hence inherently inferior schools. Academic success means attendance at a Negro state or private teachers' college, where he is taught by Negro faculty members, who are themselves products of the system. Upon graduation he returns to the ghetto to teach and perhaps prepare another generation very like himself.

Since in his experience in the United States his blackness has been a handicap, it is not surprising that the American Negro should seek some source of pride in his heritage. Important Negro figures in the sports and entertainment worlds are obvious examples. But black parents and students are also beginning to look to the schools for help. Strange to say, the older immigrants, who have had their problems with status, too, cannot seem to understand the demand for the instruction in Negro history and literature, and even Swahili, on the part of Negroes.

Hall and Burke reported the feelings and thoughts of fifteen disadvantaged New York City youth toward their schools.[1] They indicated that their schools had failed them. The curriculum was geared to white society and ignored Negro history and culture. The texts they used and the teachers who taught them were biased. The school, they added, lacked the necessary ingredients to promote their interests and prepare them to live in society. Furthermore, they concluded, the teachers were not sensitive to the needs of the students.

Weber and Motz interviewed a group of sixteen Negro male dropouts.[2] They had been enrolled in four central city schools in an eastern city where the student body was all Negro. The dropouts reported that the schools they attended were indifferent to their needs and were punitive in outlook toward them. The teaching techniques used and the content of the curriculum did not motivate the students. Furthermore, the materials used in the classroom were no inducement to the learning process. The teachers, according to these students, lacked the necessary patience and ability to clarify the subject matter taught. Also, the students had little contact with the school counselors and even less, if any, contact with the school principals.

Clark further substantiates what has been cited above.[3] In his research, he found that schools are middle class institutions with middle class aspiring teachers who teach half-truths, prejudices, and other biased concepts which are aimed at the helpless working class. The classroom, according to Clark, is basically a battlefield where a clash of cultures takes place.

The studies cited above seem to indicate that students have their own ideas about their own educations and are not always satisfied with what they receive under that name. Student evaluation should be very much a part of teacher evaluation. How can it be ignored? Although it is conceded that many students lack sound judgment and often may not see things as they really are, this limitation does not offset the fact that student responses can be helpful in many ways. The teacher and principal can get some ideas about the attitudes and reactions of the students. The students, who, after all, are the very reason for education, are seldom consulted about anything. Instead, evaluation comes from some administrative source. The students, even those in the early grades, can offer helpful suggestions, and listening to them will tend to make them feel a part of the educational process. However, student opinion on the quality of instruction is valuable only if properly interpreted. In any program of student ratings, care must be taken to avoid giving the students the impression that a teacher holds his job at their pleasure. Surely, students can be shown that their opinions are valued and respected, without turning the school over to student control.

Another problem faced by the lower class student, of which he may not even be aware, is that he has different goals in life and views them differently than does his middle class counterpart.

Vance Packard in *The Status Seekers* claims that our lower class citizens tend to be hedonists and hence are unwilling to sacrifice present for future happiness. The middle class student and his parents view education as a long drawn-out process, extending through elementary school, high school, college, and perhaps graduate or professional school. It is possibly too easy to motivate such a student. "Why should I read Shakespeare?" "Because it is required for entrance to college and you may find a question about Macbeth on an entrance examination." "Why should I study algebra?" "You have to know a lot of algebra in order to understand the space race and atomic energy." These motivations obviously refer to very distant goals.

On the other hand, lower class citizens are so concerned with immediate needs that they cannot afford the luxury of long-range planning or think in terms of remote goals. The Negro maid who gets her pay for each day's work and needs it to buy the groceries for that very day is an obvious example. The man who must pay one or two dollars every few days to have an old tire repaired because he can never get enough ahead to buy a new one is another example. Such people are natural victims of the installment plan. Their concern is not with cost, not with interest or interest rate, and not even with the number of payments, but only with the problem of meeting the payment each week. These are the workers who want to be paid weekly rather than biweekly or monthly, and they sometimes prefer to be paid in cash rather than by check. A monthly pay check would leave one of these workers penniless after the first week. It must be recognized that the goals and attitudes of such people have developed because of the inequities of our economic system as well as the policy of racial discrimination that has been perpetuated over so many years. A positive self-image and hope for the future have been in large part destroyed.

It is not surprising that the attitude of immediacy should be translated to their view of the schools. Most of the changes in curriculum have been designed by and for other groups. The introduction of science, social studies, and foreign languages in the elementary school is meaningless to the lower classes. So are the "new math" and all the other changes, called "enrichment" by the middle class educators and "frills" by the lower class student and his parents. The problem is not that the entire curriculum has no relation to lower class existence, but that even courses that could be so related are not, because the middle class teacher does not know how. The school does not have the luster for the new immigrants that it had for the old, because its curriculum is viewed as irrelevant and education is seen as a weapon in the hands of the middle class. The Negro, Puerto Rican, and Mexican-American all think of education as something that is imposed upon them by an outside force—the white Anglo-Saxon community—along with the older immigrant groups who have achieved a degree of power and influence. School attendance laws are enforced by truant officers drawn largely from the dominant community. If the newer immigrants view the education available to them as inadequate to meet their economic, social, and political aspirations, their alienation from their schools is understandable.

Of course, the adequacy of the educational job being done by urban schools is a subject of controversy, and there are conflicting opinions. Educators like John Holt, Herbert Kohl, Jonathan Kozol, and Allan C. Ornstein have severely criticized existing patterns of urban education. Kozol's book *Death at an Early Age* is about slum schools in Boston and is particularly bitter in its criticism. On the other hand, Robert J. Havighurst, professor of education at the University of Chicago and during 1967-1968 visiting professor at Fordham University, has called for a moratorium on criticism of urban schools.[4] Havighurst claims that urban schools are doing a better job than ever before. While admitting the justice of some of the accusations, he states that the schools are doing as well as any other agency of the city in dealing with problems of the poor. He considers it unreasonable that so much responsibility is placed on the schools, when so many other factors in urban life affect the situation of the poor and deprived groups. Another critic, Edgar Friedenberg, answers by agreeing that the schools are doing a "better job" today, but "in an evil undertaking that reaffirms in the slum children the poor image they've already begun to get" before coming to school.[5]

But, regardless of the views of educators, the fact is that the schools are now the subject of criticism from the slum school children and their parents as well as from educators. It does not seem possible to ignore this criticism in the hope that it will go away of itself.

The student from the lower class is frustrated not only by the curriculum and the teacher but also by the middle class students. Particularly in the high school, the lower class student, especially if he is from an ethnic or racial minority, begins to experience prejudice in the social affairs of the schools. When dating begins, considerable attention is given to the backgrounds of the boys and girls involved. The social life of the school is controlled by the middle and upper middle class students, usually with the support of the teachers and school administration. The clubs and societies of a high school seem somewhat foolish to adults, but young people can be crushed by social as well as by academic failures.

In a large northern city, a high school may be all black, but the white principal and teachers are not likely to understand the kind of clubs or social activities desired by the students. In the South, the black high school will have black teachers and a black principal, but all of them placed under a white superintendent and board of education. Also, the black principal may be so conscious of his status that he has lost touch with the students and their parents. Many of the observations of Franklin E. Frazier in *Black Bourgeoisie* apply today to black educators. The black community in the South is so conscious of the black educator's need to maintain the status quo that it is often claimed that the "Uncle Tom" concept has been replaced by "Dr. Thomas, Ph.D." And neither a black principal nor a white principal of a black high school is going to welcome a club which is the least bit militant on any issue, especially one with racial overtones.

The lower class student, be he white or Negro, has a chance to achieve status within his school by his athletic performance. In some cases the status so achieved can be community-wide. In college or university athletics it can even be nationwide. But often his status ebbs and flows as the seasons change. Vance Packard in *The Status Seekers* reports that a lower class student who is an athletic hero can date almost any girl in his school during the football or basketball season, as the case may be, but becomes a social outcast when the season is over. Packard further claims that this sudden change in status is sometimes sufficient to turn the student-athlete into a dropout. Several years ago Texas Western (now the University of Texas at El Paso) won the NCAA basketball championship with a team composed largely of Negroes. As of this date many of these black athletes have failed to graduate.[6] While they performed as athletes, they were given both financial and academic assistance. Since the completion of their athletic eligibility, they have received little aid from their university. It is no wonder that the Negro athlete and his parents view education as another area of exploitation. Although given considerable publicity, due partly to the racial content, the case at Texas Western is not unique because white lower class athletes may suffer the same fate. For this and other reasons the poor whites also tend to distrust their schools.

Thus, both the poor white and the Negro find the curriculum of the school irrelevant to their needs and tend to face social discrimination, which makes school highly unattractive to them. Furthermore, the lower class student often is able to find a job that pays a salary more than adequate for his immediate economic goals, even though the job is menial. By leaving school and entering the labor market, he can make enough money to have a car and lead a social life he finds attractive. In fact, he may make nearly as much as his father, who has had twenty or more years of experience. Nothing in his background leads him to consider that in the future he may be the first to lose his job and that he may find it difficult, in hard times, to find another. He is not likely to be concerned about his lack of opportunity for advancement, as he expects little in the way of a future, anyway.

The poor urban whites are often in direct competition with Negroes for jobs, housing, status, and, among teen-age gangs, for territory. They also live in poor neighborhoods, often in racially integrated or fringe areas. They lack the means to escape integrated schools by moving to the suburbs, as have many middle class whites, so that sometimes they send their children to parochial schools.

It is interesting to observe that when the public schools of New Orleans were finally ordered to be integrated, the white middle class school board chose two elementary schools that served the lowest class whites in the city as the first white schools in which Negro children would be enrolled. Realizing that the middle class school board had sought to comply with the federal court order in such a way that the middle class would not suffer, the whites in the integrated neighborhoods rioted. But also the enrollment in the nearby and still segregated parochial schools increased. When various agencies within the State of Louisiana, including the legislature and the governor, tried to close the public schools of New Orleans, four of the five members of the New Orleans School Board vigorously denounced this action and were determined to maintain open public schools in the city. It is interesting to observe that the fifth member of the board, Emile Wagner, who favored the closing of the public schools, was the only member of the Board who did not send his children to public schools.

Faced with the possibility of an end to public education in New Orleans, the middle class community formed an organization called Save Our Schools, or simply SOS. This organization prepared leaflets and bought television time to defend the idea of open public schools, segregated or· not. When segregationist whites near the two integrated schools attempted to physically prevent the few white children who were still trying to go to their schools from reaching their destinations, volunteers from SOS drove them to school and helped them to run the gauntlet. The aroused middle class, as well as the decisions of the federal district court, prevented the closing of the schools. Also, Emile Wagner was not re-elected to the New Orleans School Board.

In most cities, a parent can avoid having his children sent to a school outside his neighborhood and can also avoid having his children go to school with children from other neighborhoods, who have been bussed in, by sending them to parochial schools. The parent may feel that the discipline is better and the quality of education superior in parochial schools, even if he is not interested in the religious instruction. In fact, parents of one religion may send their children to schools controlled by another religious group for one of these reasons. The authors have examined the curriculum of parochial schools and the qualifications of their teachers and have found there is no basis for a claim that parochial schools offer education superior to that offered in a public school. Parochial school teachers usually deal with more crowded classes and sometimes are less qualified than even the substitute teachers in the public school system. And the lay teachers in many parochial schools are paid less than teachers in public schools, sometimes several thousand dollars per year less. But the opinion of the parent determines the school which the child attends.

Private and parochial schools as an alternative to public schools at the elementary and secondary levels are important in large cities. In New York City, only about 75 percent of the school children attend public schools, and in New Orleans, only about 50 percent. Parochial schools are designed to serve different economic levels and sometimes even different ethnic or racial groups. The New Orleans Catholic parochial schools remained segregated racially, until after the integration of the public schools was an accomplished fact. But the tuition charged varies from practically nothing to as much as five hundred dollars per year. Thus, even poor parents may send their children to parochial schools.

Such parents do not view the public schools with favor. Why, they ask, should we pay taxes to support schools that our children do not attend and then pay tuition to the schools they do attend? The unfavorable outcome of many school-bond elections in some of our cities is an indication of this negative feeling toward the public school system. The resentment can become intense if the parent of a child who attends a rather run-down parochial school sees a new, modern, and attractive public school built in his neighborhood. Sometimes the public school–parochial school antagonism is evidenced in violence among the spectators at football games between public and parochial high schools, as recently witnessed in Washington, D.C. Little seems to have been done to lessen this kind of antagonism.

Jencks has called for the establishment of private schools for black children, on the model of Catholic parochial schools.[7]

He claims that the public schools have not been able to teach black children to read and write or to add and subtract. The fault lies neither with the children nor with the schools, as such, but with the system. Racial integration was supposed to solve this problem, but it has not done so. It was claimed that more black teachers and principals would solve the problem, but even in Washington, D.C., where there are many black teachers, black children still seem unable to learn these fundamental skills. More recently, black militants have claimed that black control of schools is the answer. But Jencks claims that the few schools that are controlled entirely by blacks are not models of academic excellence. Private schools, with a curriculum frankly compensatory and remedial in character, are the solution suggested by him.

The poor Negro and white parents are alike not satisfied with the education their children receive in the city school. They both fear for the physical safety of their children in school and en route to school, and with good reason. In many schools city policemen patrol the hallways and grounds while school is in session. Furthermore, the high teacher turnover already mentioned, the assignment of a large number of inexperienced teachers, and recent teacher strikes have all combined to persuade the urban poor that the inferior academic achievement of their children, both white and Negro, is caused by defects in the schools. Dialogue between the parents of the poor and the teachers of their children needs to take place on a meaningful level. However, the life of the white middle class teacher is so different, with his different interests, different frames of reference, different value patterns, and even different vices, that he and the parent may have little to say to each other. The teacher in the ghetto school usually lives outside the school neighborhood and commutes to work, either from a suburb or nicer neighborhood. The urban poor regard him as an outsider with no stake in their community and no real interest in the children he teaches.

The Parent-Teachers Associations which are supposed to provide the means for the above-mentioned dialogue only tend to bring into focus the differences in outlook between parents and teachers. In some ghetto areas, parents hesitate to attend their meetings, fearing embarrassment due to their dress or manner of speaking. Teachers sometimes feel that they have discharged their responsibilities by four o'clock and have no interest in attending evening meetings. Often both parents in poor neighborhoods are employed, so that one or both of them must take time off from work in order to see a teacher during school hours. The consequent loss in pay causes resentment that is directed at the teacher. A monthly Parent-Teachers Association meeting would give parents and teachers an opportunity to meet in the evening.

Unfortunately, even when such meetings are well attended by both parents and teachers, the program usually does not involve matters of greatest concern to the parents. Parents sometimes become angry with teachers, because they fail to realize how little teachers can do about many of the problems of concern to the parents. Recently, the parents of the poor, particularly in Negro neighborhoods, have organized themselves and come in force to these meetings with quite militant attitudes and demands. The difficulty is to find a middle ground whereby the parents can take an enlightened, concerned interest, while still remaining able to appreciate the difficulties and problems of the teachers.

Lower class parents, especially the newest immigrants to our cities, are again raising the battle cry voiced by George S. Counts in the 1930's, when he published his classic work *Dare the Schools Build a New Social Order?*

If the urban poor view their schools as foreign and irrelevant to their needs, it might be supposed that the urban middle class is satisfied with what is given their children in the way of public education in the city. Unfortunately, middle class parents are not happy either. Although they view the needs of their children somewhat differently than do the urban poor, they feel that these needs are not being met. A number of forces, including the new Negro militance and Supreme Court decisions, have caused the urban middle class to lose some control of the urban school system. In such cases school authorities have attempted to work out some form of compromise, which turns out to be satisfactory neither to the poor nor to the middle class.

The middle class parent is primarily interested in academic programs that will prepare his child adequately for higher education. He does not support vocational and technical programs that appeal to lower class parents or into which lower class students are "dumped," as the case may be. He believes in homogeneous grouping as the surest means to provide his child with the best academic training. In some large city school systems, students are grouped into as many as seven different levels of ability. It is charged that one purpose of such grouping is the preservation of racial segregation for the upper middle and upper class students, as the highest level is nearly all white and levels become progressively more black as one moves from the highest to the lowest. Thus, it is charged, real integration exists, on other than a token level, only at about the fourth or fifth level, where the white children's parents are too low in status to protest effectively against the unwanted integration to sympathetic persons in authority.

Many of the recent outbreaks of white racism in northern cities have been among lower class and lower middle class whites, particularly those who are the children of older immigrants. These people charge that white liberals favoring school integration are middle class and expect to escape in one way or another from anything more than token integration. In turn, the Negro has reacted violently against these older immigrants.

The poor tend to favor heterogeneous grouping of students and demand that children be sent to schools outside their immediate neighborhoods, if necessary, to bring it about. Middle class parents resent both the influx of students from other neighborhoods into their schools and the removal of their children to schools in other neighborhoods. In this context, it is interesting to point out that James B. Conant, in his book *The American High School Today,* favored ability grouping of students in secondary school subjects, with the exception of such subjects as civics and physical education, and in the home-room period. Furthermore, the middle class parent feels that the curriculum under heterogeneous grouping is "watered down" to the point that lower class students can achieve success and that his children are thereby penalized.

The middle class parent can escape the problem of having his children taught in the same classroom with the children of the poor, and particularly the children of the Negro poor, by moving to the suburbs, and this desire for escape was one of the reasons cited in Chapter I for the middle class exodus to the suburbs. Without leaving the city, however, the middle class parent can avoid the problem by sending his children to private or parochial schools or even to boarding schools outside the city. Although, as mentioned above, poor parents can also send their children to parochial schools, middle class parents utilize parochial schools with higher standards and higher tuition.

The middle class parents see the schools as focusing too much attention on culturally deprived youth. Naturally they dislike paying taxes for public schools, if they send their children to private schools; but if they send their children to public schools, they resent special programs offered there that seem to be designed for disadvantaged youth. They have expressed the feeling that there has been too much emphasis on the needs of ghetto youth at the expense of their own children. Private foundations and the federal and state governments have all tended to ignore them and their needs, or so they believe. Regardless of whether this view is correct, the authors have found it to be quite prevalent among middle class parents.

The traditional view of both groups toward public schools has been that the school produces and generates democracy and that it brings together persons of differing social class, background, and means. However, at the present time residential patterns make this untrue in general, and both groups resent making it true by some arbitrary reassignment of students to schools. It is also clear that even when all classes attend the same school, they do not mix socially, and often means are found to keep them separated even in academic areas.

For example, let us examine a large public high school in a medium-sized midwestern city. The high school is old, but has been kept in good repair. It serves a rather large geographic area and enrolls some five thousand students. Of course, the student body is racially as well as socially integrated in more than a token degree. But Negro parents are not happy.

The curriculum preserves segregation, with white students taking Latin, advanced mathematics, and English courses, whereas poor whites and Negro students predominate in remedial courses and in the vocational training offered in the basement of the building. Although Negroes show up in more than proportionate numbers on the athletic teams, the members of the band that play at the games and the cheerleaders who cheer them on to victory are both almost entirely white. In fact, it took a riot on school property to make the cheerleading group even tokenly integrated. All-white clubs, as such, are not allowed, and all-black clubs are not encouraged, in part because they would find it difficult to obtain the required faculty sponsor. Of course, the city school board is almost entirely white, as are all the high-level administrators of the school system, without exception. The principal and assistant principal of this school are also white, as are the overwhelming majority of the teachers. The class officers are all white, and so are all the officers of almost all the clubs.

How do parents, both white and black, view this school? To the whites, the school is integrated. Because it is integrated, there are riots, and they fear their sons may be "beaten up" or their daughters molested while en route to or from school. They tend to oppose any expenditure for vocational or other training designed primarily to benefit black students. On the other hand, black parents regard this integrated school as a symbol of segregation, in which their children are exposed to discrimination and provocation almost daily. They believe that their children are denied fair treatment in both academic and disciplinary situations. Since they see little intermingling of their children with white children, either in or out of class, they regard the claim that the school is integrated as fraudulent. Thus, this school pleases neither white nor black parents, and no one has yet come forward with a means of dealing with a situation that is very tense at present.

Apparently integration has not really taken place at a meaningful level even in a northern high school where racial integration has been the policy for some time. However, by way of contrast, it might be well to examine a high school in a medium-sized southern city.

Although racial segregation is now illegal in public schools, this high school is still identified and identifiable as the city's Negro high school. It is named after two men who took a great deal of interest in Negro education about the turn of the century, though both were white. This high school has about fourteen hundred students, all of them Negro, but the average daily attendance is only about twelve hundred. No white students have been assigned to this school. Some Negro students have sought and been given the right to transfer to one of the city's other (white) high schools. But most of these students have returned to the Negro high school either because of social pressure or because they found the academic standards too high. It is also alleged that the parents of students seeking transfer were subjected to some economic suasion.

The building is old and not in good repair. Much of the equipment in the science laboratories and in the home economics department was transferred here when one of the other schools obtained new equipment. Much of the athletic equipment was obtained in the same way. Although this high school should be large enough to support a variety of programs, the fact is that there is little in the way of advanced mathematics, science, and other courses deemed most appropriate for the college-bound student. There is simply not much demand for this kind of curriculum.

Since this school is located in a Negro neighborhood, it could serve as a center for community activity. But it is under the control of a remote, white school board. To most of the residents of the neighborhood, this school is a symbol of Negro inferiority. Many of them, particularly the older people, accept their own inferiority as innate and no longer struggle against it; but most are not willing to accept inferiority for their children. Thus, this school enjoys little respect from its constituency.

As another example of apparent but unsuccessful integration, let us turn to an urban campus of a state university located in a large southern city. This campus was founded in the late 1950's at an abandoned military installation. Before the first student had been admitted, the campus was ordered to admit Negro students under the old "separate, but equal" doctrine, because the state did not provide a Negro institution in the city.

The first year of operation saw only token integration, with

Negroes accounting for less than 1 percent of the student population. Nevertheless violence erupted. White students painted KKK on some of the buildings. Some white students tried to force Negro students to sit in the back of classrooms. Demonstrations by both white students and citizens unconnected with the university took place. The administration acted resolutely. Access to the campus was barred to those not connected with the institution. Some students were expelled, and within a few months the campus settled down to its business in relative peace.

The following year, the state opened a branch of its Negro university in the same city. The Negro community organized a partially successful boycott of the Negro campus and its administration and faculty. In the second year of its operation, the integrated campus enrolled a student body that was nearly one-third Negro and had more than three times as many Negro students as did the Negro campus. The integration was much more than token, beginning with the second year of operation, but the problem did not end.

The students of both races were primarily graduates of the city high schools. Their attendance at this university campus was for most of them their first experience with real integration, racial or economic, since segregation kept the student bodies of the local high schools homogeneous in race and somewhat homogeneous in economic status.

The white and black students viewed each other with some degree of alarm. The white co-eds were somewhat frightened, and the white males tended to react violently to any mixed dating or even mixed boy-girl conversation. In fact, some white male students organized a vigilante committee that attacked other male students of both races who made attempts at communication across color lines. The faculty, the administration, the librarians, the counselors, all the secretarial and office help, and the campus police force were all made up entirely of white people. Some of these shared the prejudices and fears of many of the white students. The urban campus was under the control of the administration and board of trustees of the parent rural campus, and both of these groups were entirely white.

Negroes were not allowed to join any of the campus clubs,

whether social or educational, to appear in university plays, to go on educational field trips, or to represent the university in any way. White and Negro students were not allowed to eat together on campus, although no facilities other than candy machines were provided for Negroes and although there was no privately owned facility that would accommodate Negroes anywhere near the campus. This problem was not solved until the fourth year of operation and then only after the campus was ordered by a federal court to integrate its eating facilities.

Coming from inferior high schools, both parochial and public, the Negro student found himself at a disadvantage academically. He populated remedial courses in English and mathematics out of proportion to his numbers. Although placed in such courses as a result of placement examinations, it seemed to him that racial segregation was being continued when he found himself in a class with no white students. The registration procedures were complicated and confusing to the students of both races, as their parents were, for the most part, without university experience. But the black students seemed to feel more confused and remote from their previous experiences than did even the poor white students.

Most Negro and poor white students reached the campus by bus, causing the upper and upper middle class white people who lived adjacent to this campus, and who sometimes used public transportation, to resent the location of an integrated facility so close to their homes. The middle class student drove to class, but the middle class Negro student who drove to the campus ran the risk of having his tires slashed while he attended classes. The white campus police force tended to take departure from good conduct much more seriously when a Negro student was involved. White students sometimes reported cheating on the part of Negro students to the administration, and they were encouraged to make such reports.

Being denied membership in all campus clubs, including such academically oriented clubs as the French Club, Negroes attempted to organize Negro fraternities and sororities. Many of the white faculty supported the Negro students in these efforts, but the majority of the faculty, under the leadership of the administration, took the contrary view. Faculty action also prevented the organization of a Jewish sorority.

One year the administration invited students from certain high schools to come to the campus for the purpose of introducing them to the campus and university curriculum. Perhaps it was only an oversight that high schools with Negro student bodies were not invited. Later, an invitation was issued to the neglected high schools by a segment of the faculty.

Negro students often felt that the faculty discriminated against them in the assignment of grades, but such charges are very difficult to substantiate. Most observers tended to doubt their validity, although there is no doubt that white students were likely to receive much more in the way of extra assistance from some faculty members than were black students. The Negroes could bolster their charges by pointing to the black failure rate as opposed to the white failure rate. What one group took as a sure sign of discrimination, others took as convincing proof of innate inferiority. At some universities there are committees to which students can complain about unfair grading, but Negroes hesitate to make use of such committees, fearing that they will not get a fair hearing anyway and that they may make trouble for themselves in future courses. But this campus had no such committee or any other tribunal before which charges of unfair grading could be formally aired.

At this particular campus, not only the Negro but also Jewish students and faculty experienced some degree of discrimination. During the trial of Adolph Eichmann in Israel, bumper stickers and lapel buttons with the slogan, "I like Eich," were much in evidence, and one student wrote this phrase on a professor's blackboard before he arrived for class, although it was generally known that he had been imprisoned with other German Jews at Dachau. More subtle forms of discrimination in clubs and in elections were also practiced.

Just as with the high school situation described earlier, the white student and his parents viewed this campus as integrated, whereas the Negro student and his parents were acutely conscious of the separation of the races. The whites recognized that the curriculum and hence the faculty were somewhat weighted downward, that is, in the direction of more elementary courses and more junior faculty, because of the large Negro enrollment. White parents who did not recognize this fact were informed by the white administration. The Negro parent and student felt that the student's academic failures were due almost entirely either to the discrimination on this campus or to his prior segregated schooling. The inability of the Negro to take any part in the social life of the campus, even in the academic clubs, to help run the campus newspaper or yearbook, or even to appear in a play was embittering. His experience in a supposedly integrated situation did not make him feel more kindly toward whites or even acquaint him with many more whites than he had known before.

This campus has now existed for ten years, and many of its problems have been solved. Negro students can now appear in plays and, as was mentioned, can eat with their fellow students. They can no longer be denied membership in the purely academic clubs. However, it is significant that many of these improvements came only after the percentage of Negro enrollment had dropped substantially. Either because of the social discrimination or because of the higher academic standards, Negro students no longer attend the integrated campus in large numbers. Instead, they are enrolling more and more at the Negro campus in the same city—the same campus that the Negro community sought to boycott when it was originally opened. Some observers conjecture that the barriers to Negro participation at the integrated campus have been partially lifted only because the integration is now scarcely more than token. Whether or not this is true or false cannot be determined. But the conclusion that racial integration on this campus failed to achieve many of the goals of its supporters is inescapable.

The situation is not quite so bleak on urban campuses in the North, due in part to the fact that most northern campuses do not enroll a large percentage of Negro students. But there exist urban campuses in the North that claim to be integrated racially, but have few Negro students apart from those on their athletic teams. Indeed, there are cases where the only Negro student on the campus is an athlete of doubtful academic ability who was recruited solely for his athletic prowess. It is claimed in a national magazine that one such student is called "the dumb black 'jock' " by his fellow students. A black athlete who has been recruited by a university far from his home must often deal with a racial atmosphere quite different from that to which he has become accustomed, and he often finds little help in making the necessary adjustment. Just as in the high school described earlier, he may find that the athletes are black, but the cheerleaders are white. At one urban campus the black athletes threatened to refuse to play if the student body did not select some Negro cheerleaders, and the predominately white student body acceded to this demand.

Although the Negro student-athlete has certainly proved his athletic ability on more than one campus, it is easy to find discrimination even in athletics. It is claimed, and with some justice, that the Negro athlete must be even better than his white teammate if he is to be allowed to play. Further, the Negro athlete may be denied some of the awards that would come to him were he white. At one urban campus, the football award banquet failed to give any recognition to a Negro football player who had received great recognition in the national press. The resentment on the part of the black student body is understandable.

Negroes operate on the fringe of the social life of the student body, or they organize their own social life. Although the situation is changing rapidly, social fraternities and sororities still tend, in subtle ways, to deny membership to Negroes and to lower class whites. The large number of lower class students among urban campus student bodies may tend to explain further the relative unimportance of these organizations in the urban as opposed to the rural university. But, in any case, friendships are rare across racial lines. While some authorities contend that the Black Power Movement, as well as the prejudice of whites, is a barrier to interracial friendships, the authors believe that only the extremist groups in the Black Power Movement would be a deterrent influence.

At one urban campus in the Middle West, Negro students have decided to abandon attempts to integrate socially with their white fellow students. While the campus has been officially racially integrated for many years, Negro students still experience discrimination, both overt and covert, from their fellow students and from student organizations. In the fall of 1968 the Black Student Union was organized, primarily with the support of the more outstanding Negro student-athletes. Although its leader claims that this organization is "pro-Black" rather than "anti-White," there are many who see militancy in some of his statements.

One of the first moves of the Black Student Union was to organize homecoming activities for black students, separate from the general university homecoming activities, although held at the same time. Many of these activities emphasized black culture, and all of them were open to both races. In fact, financial support was sought and obtained from both white students and white faculty members, as well as from black members of the academic community. Black students have felt that previous homecoming activities were not relevant to the black students, probably because they were largely controlled by the white fraternity and sorority system. Feeling that a Negro girl could never be elected homecoming queen, the Black Student Union elected its own homecoming queen.

It is more than possible that some of the complaints of students, both white and black, are not fully justified. Still, it is important that society come to terms with the attitudes held by those most affected by the racial atmosphere of an urban university.

Sometimes the urban university alarms the community at large by its interest in projects designed to assist the poor. The Upward Bound program that exists on some urban campuses is an example, and seminars on urban problems that give attention to the needs of the poor are another. The recent conference at the University of Texas at El Paso[8] which concerned itself with Mexican-American poor did not meet with a favorable reaction from some segments of the business community, particularly the segment that owns rental housing in lower class neighborhoods of El Paso. The urban community can also become alarmed by activities of both faculty and students that appear to the community to be radical or even Communistic. Examples are "Ban the Bomb" marches, peace vigils, and, in the South, sit-ins and other demonstrations having to do with civil rights. A student organization known as Students for a Democratic Society has been under particular attack. The administration and faculty at one midwestern urban university learned during the academic year 1967–1968 that the city police had infiltrated the local chapter of SDS. Several months after this infiltration was reported to the press, the university senate mildly condemned such actions, but the administration took no public stand. The police defended their right to infiltrate certain organizations and made it clear that this practice would be continued. One of the student members alleged that a police official told him that "this community will not tolerate an organization such as yours."

In other cities, officials of state and city government have hired student spies not only to infiltrate student organizations but also to report on their professors. The Louisiana State Sovereignty Commission was particularly active in this regard during the early 1960's.

The new importance and increased number of community colleges has been discussed elsewhere. The community college draws a much larger proportion of its student body from the lower economic classes and from racial and ethnic minority groups than does even the urban university. The reasons are obvious. The community college generally charges less or no tuition, has lower entrance requirements, and offers terminal vocational programs of greater interest to lower class groups. Many members of the middle class view these projects as wasteful, since they plan to send their children to either the urban or a rural university. They may also claim, with some justice, that the faculty of the local community college is not very good and feel that the whole enterprise is fraudulent. On the other hand, a middle class parent may decide to send his son or daughter to the local community college if he doubts his or her academic ability or interest.

So far we have examined urban education from the point of view of the student and his parents. But the teachers themselves have attitudes that cannot be ignored. Teachers are becoming more militant. Because many of them feel that the normal professional organizations lack sufficient power to gain desirable goals, the American Federation of Teachers is becoming more powerful, in spite of the opposition of some other groups. Teachers not only are interested in their own economic well-being but are demanding some voice in educational decision making.

In the past many teachers were treated very much like the other employees of the school. They were not consulted on the appointment of their principal or colleagues. Even today, some states do not have provisions for the tenure of teachers. When hired, a teacher was often assigned to teach classes without regard to his interests or capabilities. Usually, a teacher had no influence in the selection of texts for his own classes and certainly no voice in formulating the general curriculum of his school. He may have been assigned many noninstructional duties, such as ticket taking at school games or, in other ways, assisting with extracurricular activities.

But today teachers see themselves as professional educators involved with the many aspects of urban education. They are demanding that they be consulted on a wide variety of the problems which face urban schools. Many teachers have themselves come to see the irrelevancy of much that is being taught and are demanding that changes be made to accommodate the needs of the diverse student bodies that made up the schools. Teachers are no longer willing to placidly accept decisions on curricular matters and textbooks that are made in the state capital, often by politicians who are not educators and who may have some goals in mind that are not related to good education.

The shortage of teachers at all levels, as well as the difficulty of the problems involved, has made school administrations more willing to listen to their faculties than ever before. Also, teachers have found that they can exercise power if they are well organized. Teachers now lobby in state capitals as effectively as many other groups.

Teachers are interested in such things as class size and teaching loads, but they are also concerned with the physical facilities with which they must work. They are demanding more and more up-to-date equipment. The meetings of their professional societies as well as their professional journals have let them know what is now available in the way of teaching aids. It should be no surprise to anyone that informed teachers should demand that they be allowed to use the most modern equipment obtainable.

In recent years the subject-matter knowledge of teachers in service has been severely questioned by both lay and professional critics. Universities, and particularly urban universities, have set up programs to enable teachers to obtain fresh training in their disciplines. The National Science Foundation has established many programs, including In-Service Institutes, Summer Institutes, and Academic Year Institutes, to enable teachers of mathematics and the sciences to learn of the recent advances in their fields. More recently, the Office of Education has provided similar programs to aid teachers in other disciplines. Many states now require that teachers take refresher courses every few years in order to keep their certificates in force. Professional organizations for each of several different disciplines have been formed especially to aid elementary and secondary school teachers, and these are now larger and more active than ever before.

Teachers are better prepared now than at any time in our previous history. More of them have advanced degrees, and more of them have recent training. They are no longer content to "obey orders," but are demanding that they be treated as the professionals they are. To an extent the new teacher militancy conflicts with the new parent and student militancy, but the result of both will be a lessening of the arbitrary power of the school administration. As long as communication can be maintained among the students, the parents, the teachers, and the higher levels of administrations, the schools cannot help but profit from the ideas of all these groups.

While the teachers, the students, and their parents would seem to be the people most involved with the schools, the urban community at large also has a stake in the elementary, secondary, and higher educational institutions, which all segments of the community help to support. The business community offers or fails to offer employment to the graduates of the schools, the trade-unions offer or fail to offer membership to them, and the citizens of the community look to these young people to provide future responsible leadership for the city. Since today our young people seek to further their careers through study, the needs of local employers in the light of available education must be examined.

It is becoming increasingly apparent that graduation from high school is prerequisite to most kinds of employment in cities. Negroes tend to regard this as another method of discriminating against them, since high school graduation would seem to have little relation to some jobs for which it is required. Negroes, and other minority groups, also tend to resent the aptitude and psychological tests which some employers now require, tending to feel that such tests are designed to screen out all but the white middle class citizens. Although the actual knowledge gained in high school may not be necessary for a particular position, employers offer considerable statistical evidence to support their claim that high school dropouts do not make good employees. It is alleged that their absenteeism is higher, they are more accident-prone, and they present a less favorable appearance and are less co-operative than high school graduates. Most employers are not impressed by the fact that Abraham Lincoln had, perhaps, less than three years of formal education. Although they would not want to be quoted, many employers and personnel directors state quite frankly that they consider the high school dropout to be unreliable even for menial employment. On the other hand, higher educational requirements for positions can only be enforced when the labor supply is large relative to the number of positions.

One result has been that an ever growing percentage of young people now graduate from high school, in spite of the considerable attention devoted to the problem of the dropout. Of course, one reason is that high school education is now more available, partly because of the growing urbanization in this country. But it is also charged that the curriculum is now less demanding than formerly. Whether or not this charge has a basis in fact, it is accepted by many employers. Employers claim that today's high school graduate is deficient in the three R's and that his dress, appearance, punctuality, and manners are all below acceptable levels. The business community is likely to view the high school as a production center that turns out the product with which it can fill its lower-echelon positions. The high school graduates will be the clerks, typists, messenger boys, and so on, but they are likely to command no real respect. In fact, the city business leaders are likely to live in suburbs partly because they lack confidence in the high schools of the central city, as has been pointed out.

It might be mentioned that some employers tend to show a slight preference for the graduates of parochial high schools. These have presumably been exposed to superior discipline and education and have usually been required to dress in ways that are more likely to meet with adult approval. The boys, for example, may have been required to wear neckties to school. However, this prejudice in favor of the parochial graduate is far from being universal.

Lacking respect for the present high school graduate, many employers are now demanding at least some college background in applicants for certain positions that were formerly filled by high school graduates. One result is an increased demand for higher education, which has been responsible for the growth of urban universities and community colleges. Unfortunately, some educators now fear that eventually employers will demand college graduates to fill many positions for which college degrees are unnecessary, so that the colleges may be forced to lower their academic standards, just as high schools have already done. Worse, other educators feel that this lowering of standards has already taken place in the community colleges and urban universities, at least. Employers, however, sometimes claim that they can fill their needs at a certain level with college graduates, that college graduates perform better, and that they can be more easily advanced or sent through training programs, even though they do not need college training in their initial positions. Employers who fail to hire all the college graduates they feel they need sometimes refer to their competitors' practice of hiring college graduates, when not absolutely necessary, as "stockpiling talent." In any case, industries can fill some of their positions with persons who have attended either the local university or community college.

In many medium-sized cities, the largest employer is often the local branch of a corporation with home offices in another part of the country. The local branch manager and probably his chief assistants, as well, are hired by the home office, which is not so likely to hire graduates of the local university. Usually the highest level of personnel will be graduates of one of the more prestigious universities in the East. But the local university graduate can reasonably hope to move into the second level of responsibility.

Some industries view the local university not only as a source from which to obtain university graduates but as a place where their regular employees can undertake further study. The presence of an urban university is an important factor in persuading an industry to locate one of its operations in a given city. This company is almost certain to mention the availability of study at the local university in its recruitment campaigns and even in its proposals for government contracts. Often the company will pay all or part of the tuition of one of its employees who undertakes advanced study in an area related to the company's operations, and it may give the employee some time off for study or readjust his hours of employment to make such study possible. Sometimes a local company will establish scholarships, graduate fellowships, and even endowed chairs at the local university and make available some of its facilities to the students and faculty for research purposes. The company may even give grants or research contracts to faculty members or groups of faculty members. It is not surprising that the university tends to develop strength in the academic areas most closely related to the interests of local industries.

Most large cities have a great number of various kinds of schools that are designed to prepare citizens, usually high school graduates, for particular positions. These institutions are usually profit-making enterprises, such as business colleges, beauty colleges, drafting colleges, and institutions offering training in electronics or automobile mechanics. Since such a school must be able to place its graduates if it is to stay in business, it usually offers a very narrow curriculum that is designed to prepare a student for a specific position. These institutions are, then, the direct opposite of the usual college or university, with its liberal arts tradition. Private business colleges, as well as the community colleges, teach typing, shorthand, bookkeeping, business machines, and data processing. If they teach English or composition, they call this material "business English" or "business letter writing." They maintain close contact with businesses that employ a large number of secretaries, clerks, and typists. Sometimes they even operate employment bureaus for their graduates, which businesses find convenient to use. Often, these employment bureaus can even arrange for part-time employment for their students while the students are finishing the program. The more technical schools maintain contact with the larger companies, and those who do not produce graduates satisfactory to these employers do not long survive.

As with other profit-making enterprises, this field has also attracted a fair number of fakes. These schools prey upon the ignorant and uninformed and, in particular, on the high school dropout. Such schools take their students' money and give them nothing in return. They do not make good on their promises of job placement. Naturally, such schools cannot stay in business very long, but they often succeed in making a great deal of money for their promoters and in doing incalculable damage to the image of education before they fold. Some of the frauds are mail-order or correspondence schools, although there exist correspondence schools of genuine value.

Since their founding, American labor unions have always supported public education. Today many teachers in large cities, in the elementary and secondary schools and even in the colleges, belong to the American Federation of Teachers. There have been teacher strikes for better wages and working conditions, and the more traditional trade-unions have supported the American Federation of Teachers with both money and sympathy. But labor unions have unfortunately given only lip service in support of technical and vocational education, an area which it might be supposed would concern them most. While some unions give scholarships to colleges, they show little interest in the establishment of co-operative programs with high schools or community colleges, whereby a student might learn a trade. They tend to require the same period of apprenticeship of young people, whether or not they have successfully completed appropriate vocational training in a school. They usually offer no assistance in the placement of graduates of vocational programs, particularly where these graduates are members of minority groups. It seems clear that trade-unions do not really value vocational training. It also seems clear that unions are becoming alienated from the new urban poor, the Negro and Puerto Rican groups, and that they will not view with approval efforts on the part of the schools to assist these groups to move into the skilled trades.

It is no surprise that there should be diverse views as to the quality of the schools in a city by all the many and diverse elements that make up the city. The problem of urban education is not that some segments of the city population are not satisfied, but rather that almost all segments seem to find the schools unsatisfactory for one reason or another. Since the public schools rely on the public for support, something must be done to enable the city schools to achieve a more favorable image. It has become trite to say that today's youth is tomorrow's citizenry, but truth is often trite. When the teen-ager of today leaves school because he finds it of no value to him, we must remember that later he will be the taxpayer and parent whose negative feelings toward the schools cannot be ignored. No proposal for solution has yet been advanced which has gained wide support. But school boards should be hard at work exploring possibilities and communicating with all segments and levels of the city's population. That the school boards of many cities are undertaking any such activity can surely be doubted.

NOTES

[1]Beatrice M. Hall and Nelson S. Burke, "Some Disadvantaged Youths Look at Their Schools," *Journal of Negro Education*, XXXVII (Spring, 1968), 136–137.

[2]George H. Weber and Annabelle B. Motz, "School as Perceived by the Dropout," *Journal of Negro Education*, XXXVII (Spring, 1968), 127–134.

[3]Kenneth B. Clark, *Dark Ghetto* (New York: Harper and Row, 1965), p. 1.

[4]New York *Times*, January 28, 1968, p. 56.

[5]*Ibid.*

[6]Jack Olsen, "The Black Athlete," Part III, *Sports Illustrated*, July 15, 1968, 28–43.

[7]New York *Times*, November 3, 1968, Magazine Section, p. 30.

[8]*The Texas Observer*, October 13, 1967, pp. 1–3.

CHAPTER VII

Adult Education for Social Change in the Urban Community

The cities of our nation cannot survive and continue to make a contribution to our total national life unless the adults who live, work, and spend their leisure hours in the metropolis can work together to explore the avenues that would lead to the changes so urgently needed. Because of the number, the seriousness, and the nature of the problems that beset our cities, grass-roots, informal instruction of the undereducated adult population is a necessity. However, the educated population of the urban complex cannot be ignored, and they, too, must be exposed to the massive effort of re-education. This task is not a simple one.

There appear to be several areas of greatest urgency that must be dealt with if the gap between urban and suburban living is going to be narrowed. Racial tension, although it permeates all segments of American life, rural as well as urban, must be alleviated in the big cities, or there is danger that our cities will become battlegrounds. This alleviation of tension can come about only by changes in the social attitudes and the behavior of the people of the metropolis, as well as by changes in the legal structure. The passage of fair housing and fair employment ordinances is important, but far from sufficient alone. Adults usually have a relatively fixed system of values, which is difficult to change by some formal course of instruction. The whole concept of producing changes in attitudes and behavior patterns among urban citizenry needs to be studied further.

Adult education has been important for some years. Johnstone, in one of a series of studies sponsored by the National Opinion Research Center, found that approximately twenty-five million Americans were active in some form of adult education during

116

the period from June 1, 1961, to May 31, 1962.[1] The typical participant was young and well educated and lived in an urban area. Johnstone predicts an enormous increase in adult education activity, with emphasis on learning for work, learning for leisure, and liberal education. Hopefully, there will be some emphasis on social change as well.

Perhaps in the course of the everyday lives of the poor, consumer education is the most important area of concern. Our schools have treated this subject superficially in the past and have not been willing to get down to some of the unpleasant aspects of our free enterprise system. Furthermore, too little has been done by the local, state, and federal governments to protect low income consumers. Our low income urban dwellers have been at the mercy of the small loan companies with high interest rates. They are also victimized by installment purchase plans. Not being able to afford an attorney and not knowing where they might obtain free legal advice, the poor do not effectively defend their rights. They buy inferior food in their neighborhood stores, whether locally owned or branches of chains.

The middle class consumer is more easily able to travel about the city and make price comparisons, but the low income consumer must bear the brunt of discriminatory pricing practices. Sometimes the poor are called stupid or lazy because they do not "shop around," but the poor are not cosmopolitan even though they have lived in urban centers for most of their lives. They are the products of poor educational systems, and a good number are school dropouts. Some are Spanish-speaking and have never learned to read, write, speak, or understand English well. Some are unemployed or even unemployable functional illiterates, living in impoverished conditions. Combined, these qualities do not make for an enlightened consumer.

Modest programs such as the one conducted at St. Jerome's School in the Bronx, New York City, designed to enhance and develop community understanding of budgeting, credit, and nutrition, will help to alleviate some of the problems that the new immigrants to our cities face. The bilingual approach in this program is an added feature which will serve to attract some Spanish-speaking citizens who might not otherwise attend. Baby sitters are provided for participants with young children.

The middle class citizen often does not fare well in the market place either. The outcry that has produced a Truth in Lending Act mentioned earlier came from middle class voices primarily. Battles over honest packaging rage in Congress every few years. Several years ago an experiment was conducted in California, in which housewives were asked to buy certain standard household items at the lowest per unit cost. The problem was to decide whether it was better to buy a fourteen-ounce can of beans for twenty-one cents or a fifteen-ounce can for twenty-three cents, among many others. Although every one of these women was a college graduate, not one of them achieved a perfect score, and less than half scored 50 percent or better.

The magazine *Consumer Reports*, published monthly by Consumers Union, a nonprofit consumers' organization, gives information on such matters as well as on laws introduced in or passed by Congress. In each issue there is a section called the "Docket" in which are described legal actions against fraudulent wholesale or retail operations. Here it is found that one company packs only fifteen ounces in a container that claims to contain sixteen ounces. Or one reads of a meat company that puts decomposed and vermin-infested meat into its hamburger or sausage. Endless fraudulent money-making schemes, often using the mail, are described. The situation is all the more shocking when it is recognized that only legal actions are reported. How much dishonesty passes unnoticed and does not lead to legal action is a matter for speculation. But when one reads of the smallness of the fines that have been levied against some of our largest corporations for so dangerously tampering with the public health as well as with the public pocketbook, one feels unsafe indeed.

Consumer Reports appeals primarily to the middle class, but is probably read only by a minority of even this group. The corporations go on and on demanding the right to regulate themselves and repeating the slogan *caveat emptor*. There was some sense to this slogan before the days of prepackaged foods, but it makes little sense now. And if one recalls the demand by the General Electric Company that electric companies be allowed to regulate themselves, which came almost immediately after these companies were caught in their little game of "monopoly" and price fixing, one can easily see that everyone can use some governmental protection from these corporations at one time or another. But consumer economics courses are not often taught either in our high schools or in our colleges, so that even the relatively educated public does not demand the needed legislation with sufficient force.

Since educational institutions have failed to provide consumer education, a massive campaign by local media and nonprofit business organizations must be initiated to improve the city dwellers' understanding of the consumer market place. No longer can we tolerate an economic arena that to all intents and purposes is just as wicked now as in the days of the so-called "Robber Barons." The large legitimate businesses of our cities have an obligation to lead the way so that the urban resident, especially if he be poor, can be a productive and informed member of the consumer community.

The business community can help the slum dweller in other ways. The Urban Coalition, which is a national alliance of business, labor, and civil rights leaders, enlists the resources of private business and industry to fight slum problems. The New York branch, founded about two years ago, has four million dollars in resources. It has established the Coalition Venture Corporation, which makes soft loans to businessmen from minority groups in slum areas, and the Coalition Development Corporation, which offers technical assistance to small slum businesses. Small businesses often fail because the entrepreneur cannot get competent advice quickly enough. The Urban Coalition will help to increase the number of neighborhood businesses in slum areas and so relieve the tension often caused by the presence of slum neighborhood stores and shops owned by suburban dwellers.

In the beginning of the Industrial Revolution, many men worked twelve hours a day for six or seven days a week. When the forty-hour week became more or less standard, some attention was focused on the use of leisure time. Now it appears likely that men will work even less than forty hours per week in the not too distant future. How will they spend their leisure time? Some workers will spend part of it by commuting to work over longer distances, but the poor of the inner city will not have the problem of commuting. Education for leisure time was one of the early purposes of education, when education was only for the rich or leisure class. Our leisure class is now shrinking, and some would even claim that it no longer exists.

But what of the poor? They have had no education for leisure time. The young men who are seen standing on our street corners obviously do not know how to use their time for constructive purposes. Bernstein has stated, "Leisure time must be an integral aspect of work time, else we forfeit civilization and become a producing society, not a productive society."[2] However, there must be jobs that will provide the necessary inducements to promote this attitude. Also, the urban community must provide low-cost leisure-time activities and make these available to the poor. Adult education has a large role in promoting leisure-time activities. Adult education centers could give instruction in bowling or other sports accessible to adults. They could give instruction in various forms of dancing. Discussion sessions on the issues of the day could be organized and some information disseminated otherwise than by means of formal instruction.

Adult education is also needed in the area of politics and government. In a democracy, it would be supposed that the right to vote would be of paramount importance to the citizens. However, in the United States, we observe that in most elections less than 50 percent of the citizens eligible to vote actually do so. In purely local elections, the percentage is often very much smaller. The United States has one of the worst records of voter participation of any democracy in the world. Political scientists claim that our ballots are too long, that our voters are asked to vote for candidates to too many offices. The duties of many of these offices are only vaguely understood by many voters. Even immediately after casting his vote, the average voter cannot tell for whom he has voted for the office of Treasurer of State and may not be able to tell whether or not such an office as Treasurer of State even exists. Short of governmental reform, which does not appear to be in prospect, voter education would seem an absolute necessity if democracy is to continue to function. Social change can come about only if those who desire social change can make their wishes known at the ballot box.

The labor market may be totally foreign to the poor urban resident. He may not know what kinds and types of jobs he should seek or which are available. Federal and state employment agencies render considerable assistance, but they often do not know how to help the lower class worker sell himself to an employer. Advertisements placed in local papers by employment agencies seem to describe the applicant's skills and employment aspirations in what must be his own terms. Often, these are not the terms designed to appeal to a prospective employer. Here, real education as to employment opportunities, job benefits paid for by the employer, and job security must be made available.

Adults who live in ghettos need to be exposed to the resources of the community. What are the agencies and bureaus in the city to which the ghetto dweller can look for assistance? Does he know about the Housing Authority, the Legal Aid Society, and so on? If not, the means must be found to give him this kind of information.

One group that is often neglected in discussions of adult education is the older or senior citizens of the community. Many of these people live on fixed incomes, and their purchasing power has shrunk greatly in recent years. They face the prospect of further shrinkage of purchasing power in the years ahead. The periodic increases in social security benefits and in particular the newly enacted medical benefits render some financial assistance, but the elderly still have much leisure and little money to spend on nonessential leisure activities. Many old people find that they have dropped from the middle class status of their middle years to a subsistence poverty level. They can still enjoy some activities, if these can be provided them at little or no cost. They could also make a contribution to the education of other citizens if there were a means by which their considerable talents could be utilized. Hopefully, programs of adult education will not neglect this growing percentage of the population.

What are the agencies that should provide adult education in the urban community? One naturally thinks first of the schools, both private and public, including the urban community colleges and universities. High schools often offer courses of instruction of interest to adults. At one time, many large city high schools taught English as well as technical courses to foreign-born adults. Urban universities often have divisions of continuing education, which provide a variety of opportunities in adult education.

Urban extension centers of Indiana University offer courses in a division of continuing education in the areas of applied arts, applied commerce, English language and literature, history and religion, foreign languages, and mathematics. During the academic year 1968–1969, courses were offered to provide increased employment opportunities, as well as to enrich the lives of the participants. Of particular interest were the courses designed to prepare students for the real estate examination and the courses in income tax return preparation.

The Division of Continuing Education at Wichita State University in Wichita, Kansas, offers a variety of programs of interest to the adult community. In particular, efforts have been made to attract adult women whose children have grown and left them with leisure. Many of these women need to have their skills in a variety of fields updated, so that they can return to full-time employment. Others may wish to cultivate music, writing, or other avocations which the demands of their families have forced them to neglect for many years. Many former teachers wish to return to the profession after their children are grown, but need to revalidate their teaching certificates. Five hundred people participated in the program during the academic year 1968–1969.

Unfortunately, some urban universities have made no attempt to offer any program in adult education. The high schools seem to have less commitment to adult education than formerly, and there is considerable resistance to such programs on the part of many in education circles.

In any case, the schools cannot tackle this job alone, partly because they seem inherently to be dedicated to the preservation of the status quo. Also, as has been mentioned repeatedly, many of our citizens have lost faith in the schools and feel alienated from them. The young man who dropped out of school because he found the curriculum irrelevant to his life is not likely to return to that same school for adult education. All agencies of the city, state, and nation have a stake in the solution to the problem of urban adult education and must make some contribution to it.

City libraries also further adult education, not only by providing educational resources and some assistance in their use but also by offering more formal courses of instruction. Libraries have sponsored "Great Books" and other programs. They have presented lecture series on such topics as the "New Math" and on political and social questions. Patrick Penland, in a doctoral dissertation written at the University of Michigan during 1960–1961, reports that the librarian is the key to the commitment or lack of commitment to adult education in American public libraries. In a study by the American Library Association conducted during 1963, racial segregation was found to be an important barrier to the effective use of a library for adult education. This study reports that direct discrimination was confined to sixteen states, but that indirect racial discrimination was found in libraries throughout the United States. Unfortunately, other studies have shown that some adult education projects sponsored by libraries have been of greatest interest to well-educated, socially active young adults of high social and economic status. Thus, it may be that libraries, as well as schools, tend to discriminate against the poor and minority groups in their programs.

Labor-union locals have been active in educational programs for their members, particularly in the field of politics. Labor leadership seeks to keep union members informed on impending legislation that affects unionization, industrial safety, and other such matters of interest to labor. Often the political action arm of a labor union provides information concerning the candidates for public office and their views on matters affecting labor. But unions may also provide job training and opportunities in more traditional academic subjects.

The local YMCA or YWCA or CYO may provide many opportunities for education. Often courses in dancing, bridge, chess, and other leisure-time activities are offered. Usually instruction in one or more sports is available to adults as well as to children. Sometimes these organizations sponsor special-interest clubs, or such clubs may exist separately from any parent organization. Examples are "radio ham" clubs, coin and stamp collecting clubs, hiking clubs, chess clubs, and the like. Usually these clubs offer instruction to the neophyte, as well as providing opportunities for adults already possessing a degree of knowledge and skill.

Some businesses and industries offer training for employment opportunity. Industries have recently sought and obtained government support for this purpose. Radio and television provide many educational opportunities for the adult in his own home. Most large cities have an educational television station, which may offer programs of general educational value as well as more formal courses of instruction, sometimes with college credit, in a variety of fields. There is, however, some criticism of the television industry for not moving ahead faster in the field of education.

In the Negro sections of some cities, educational programs involving Negro history and culture have been initiated. These newer immigrants to our cities have followed the example set by the Jewish immigrants to New York many years ago and have established their own "schools" in vacant stores and elsewhere, to teach the material of interest to them. Courses in Black Culture and in Swahili were begun in the Watts section of Los Angeles shortly after the riots in that city.

Private foundations and agencies of government have instituted instructional programs having to do with problems of segregation and integration. When such programs have involved group discussions, as well as formal lectures, an easing of racial tensions and understanding across racial lines have taken place. Hopefully, more such programs will be inaugurated in the future. But it is difficult to reach the persons in the community who most need to be reached.

City government itself can and should provide some educational opportunity for the adult population. The Human Resources Administration of New York City co-ordinates that city's antipoverty programs through community corporations and planning committees in twenty-five poverty areas. This agency supervises the allocation of more than thirty million dollars for five hundred year-round community action programs, which include attention to adult education in these areas.

The educational needs of the adult urban population require further study. Perhaps each city should assign to one of its agencies the task of examining the need in this area and making recommendations. Many agencies within the community can contribute, but they may need some co-ordination. It would seem to be the responsibility of city government to provide it.

NOTES

[1]Robert C. Clarke and Edward B. Sasse, "The Adult Education Enterprise," *Review of Educational Research*, XXXV (June, 1965), 169.

[2]Abraham Bernstein, *Education of Urban Populations* (New York: Random House, 1967), p. 309.

CHAPTER VIII

Prospects in the Decade Ahead

In the previous chapters some of the problems of urban education have been examined. It should be remembered that there are many cities in the United States whose problems may differ due to their geographic locations. The authors have attempted to make some generalizations about all our cities and to give some specific examples of situations in cities in the South, West, and Middle West, as well as in those of the East. As cities in all parts of our country have so many problems that seem almost to defy solution, what can be said for the future?

The percentage of urban population classified as poor will continue to grow, partly because the flight of the middle class to the suburbs will continue. Today, it is claimed that one-third of the New York City population can be called poor. It is predicted that by 1970 this proportion will rise to one-half. The upper class and some of the upper middle class will continue to live in isolated islands of luxury in the inner city, but their importance as a political force will continue to decline. Housing will still be a problem for the urban poor, but many more units will be built by means of federal or state aid as well as by private enterprise.

The poor, and especially members of minority groups, will gain a larger role in the operation of their schools, either through increased representation on the city school board or through neighborhood leadership discussed earlier. Elizabeth Koontz, former President of the National Education Association, strongly approved the principle of decentralization and urged a "return to the individual schools and the separate publics they serve of their rightful share of authority and responsibility for operating schools." The National Education Association now claims to have a multifaceted program directed toward the urban school problem, reaching from preschool programs to adult education. Mrs. Koontz has described the New York City decentralization plans as "little short of bedlam" and a "mad scramble for power and influence." In the future, the leadership of the National Educational Association and the American Federation of Teachers will probably be consulted on school decentralization plans.

Racial tension will continue to be an important factor in urban life. The struggle for leadership in the Negro community will continue. Gradually the more militant leaders will triumph, and the older organizations, such as the National Association for the Advancement of Colored People, will go on losing members and influence. Young black people see progress toward their goals as too slow under the old leaders, some of whom, they feel, may have "sold out." The consequences of the assassination of Martin Luther King, Jr., will long be felt. The dilemma is that the Black Power Movement has turned away from the old black leaders' and white liberals' fight for integration. Now black schools and other black institutions, under the control of black people, are being demanded. C. Shelby Rooks, Executive Director of the Fund for Theological Education, Princeton, New Jersey, could hardly be called a black militant. But in a speech delivered at a conference in Princeton in the spring of 1968, he well expressed the frustration and anger of many black people in the United States. According to Rooks, the typical American Negro views American society as racist and places the blame for this condition of society on all white people, including those who have been active in support of Negro Civil Rights. The American Negro cannot believe that the average white is as unaware as he probably is of the conditions of Negro life in this country. Fearing and distrusting white society, what could be more natural than that the Negro demand an opportunity to create for himself a community of his own? But integration of urban schools and other areas of urban life will continue. Black people will increasingly gain entrance into corporations and universities, neighborhoods and churches, and clubs and professional societies, which have been white or nearly white in the past. All these institutions will, to an extent, be remolded by the influx of black people, just as in the past they have been remolded by the influx of older immigrants.

State and private universities, both urban and rural, will offer special programs to prepare teachers and administrators for urban school positions at the undergraduate and graduate levels. Doctoral programs in urban education will become more and more popular, but the chief emphasis will be on the preparation of the urban school teacher. As Harry N. Rivlin, Dean of Fordham's School of Education, said:

> There are those who pronounce *era* as though it were error. If we are to have a new era in urban education rather than just a new error, we must have expert teachers. Unless the urban schools do develop the expert teachers they need, with the increased funds that are available, we shall be heading for a great disillusionment, with disastrous results for the schools, the cities, and the nation.[1]

As more state legislatures establish urban universities, these institutions can be expected to assume the special responsibility of developing relations with the urban community. A concept of community service through their various undergraduate, graduate, and professional programs will become manifest and will make significant contributions to the life of the city. The private urban colleges and universities will also have to meet their professional commitments to the city.

It is only logical that our colleges and universities located in the heart of the metropolitan areas should be vitally concerned and involved with the problems of urban education. How can they remain detached? All urban institutions must develop new programs to meet grass-roots needs. Effective preparation of those who will live and work in the city of the future is so urgently needed that the urban universities must attach great importance to this role. Programs must be continuously evaluated and modified as necessary to meet the urban challenge.

School, college, and university staffs will need to study innovations to determine which are worthy of emulation. Past experience alone is not sufficient to deal with new problems. For example, information about work-study programs, adult education programs, programed learning and machine teaching, other technological innovations, departmentalization in the elementary grades, the teaching of English to non-English-speaking people, and in many other areas needs to be shared with professors and school personnel alike.

Schools and universities, in co-operation with community groups, will need to establish resource centers to collect materials and data of interest to all. A community resource center could also serve as a clearinghouse for educational and vocational opportunities. Such a center would be the focal point where the university, school, and community can pool their resources to construct programs to meet the needs of urban youth.

More and more research money will be available to universities from both private foundations and governmental sources for the purposes of studying urban problems and urban school problems. In the past much of this money has been wasted on ivory-towered schemes, with little in the way of positive results. Recently, the Ford Foundation gave Harvard University and the Massachusetts Institute of Technology three million dollars each for the purpose of studying urban problems. Probably this money will be used to finance projects of professors and graduate students at these two rich and prestigious institutions. The impact that this six million dollars could have on the slums of Boston, if applied to the establishment of training programs or to the building of better housing, is incalculable. The anger of slum dwellers at such programs is understandable. They have been studied enough. What they want is help.

The struggle between the research and teaching functions of a university will continue. As more and more of the research is "sponsored" either by private corporations or by agencies of the United States government, the danger that university professors will lose their independence will increase. Administrators and professors have already established their own companies, which sometimes even do business with the university. Occasionally distinguished professors from our greatest universities testify, supposedly as disinterested, expert witnesses, at congressional hearings. But investigation reveals that these professors are often on the payroll of companies having vital interests in the outcome of the hearings. Ridgeway[2] lists the high officers of universities who serve on university boards of trustees and might consequently seek to guide the research efforts of their universities in directions of particular interest to certain industries. Worse, they may discourage publication of research results that are inimical to companies in which they have interests.

Students have discovered many of the financial connections of their professors and have reacted unfavorably in the past. Particularly, as the teaching, especially the teaching of undergraduates, is left more and more to teaching assistants, the students are coming to demand a voice in the administration of their universities. Their youthful idealism is shattered by the discovery that the professors are unavailable to them, not because they are engaged in a lofty search for Truth for its own sake, but because they are engaged in nonteaching activity which has high financial rewards. At many universities, the students are gaining some voice in their own destinies, and they will gain more in the future.

Ridgeway also charges that many of the government scientists, fearing that eventually peace will be restored, are now trying to apply some of the war technology to the problems of the city, such as techniques to control mob action. But they are also seeking to apply computer technology and systems analysis to the problems of the city and even to teaching, although with indifferent results.

Almost any method of instruction that promises to teach more students with fewer teachers is certain to gain a hearing. Universities are becoming as cost-conscious as other large organizations. Can machines teach? How about programed learning, which does not require a live teacher? Can lectures be taped or filmed and then used over and over again? Closed-circuit television is already proving valuable on many campuses, and its use will increase. The manufacturers of all these devices are very active in attempting to convince universities that these media are as effective as or even more effective than more traditional modes of instruction. However, the major emphasis is on decreasing cost. Sometimes it happens that the use of machinery is more expensive than anticipated, so that costs are higher rather than lower. But once a university has been sold on machinery and sold machinery, it is very difficult to return to old patterns. But learning machines can only support and not replace the teacher, if effective instruction is to be maintained.

Even elementary schools and secondary schools have not escaped contact with computer technology. Many high schools now teach some data processing, and the number of such high schools will grow, particularly in cities in which are located industries with large computer installations. But attempts are being made to teach more traditional parts of the curriculum with computers as well.

The curriculum in our schools has undergone considerable change in the recent past, and indications are that change will continue and even accelerate. Dr. Robert Davis, Director of the Madison Mathematics Project at Syracuse University and Webster College and a leading innovator in the teaching of mathematics, feels that the real revolution in mathematics education has not yet taken place, for all the talk about the new math. In 1967, American students represented the United States in an international mathematics competition involving twelve well-developed nations. The United States entry did not fare very well. Davis claims that one difficulty is that our teaching techniques have not kept pace with the new curriculum. He feels that other countries, England particularly, have been more successful in developing superior teaching techniques and in getting them implemented in classrooms. Unfortunately, Davis speaks of eighth-graders studying what is now considered university-level mathematics. One must suppose that he is thinking of the superior student, and not of one who might be labeled "socially disadvantaged."

Dr. Max Beberman of the University of Illinois Committee on School Mathematics (UICSM), on the other hand, is interested in the development of special mathematics programs of a remedial character, as well as of college preparatory programs. His most recent book (in comic-book form, by the way) is an attempt to teach seventh-graders the fractions that they failed to learn in the fifth and sixth grades. Much of the UICSM material is so untraditional that it incites criticism as well as praise, but it seems to work wherever it has been given an honest trial.

Changes in content and teaching techniques are also on the horizon in other disciplines. There are those who charge that our teacher training institutions do not really teach anybody to teach, but that most children have so strong a desire to learn that they learn in spite of the teaching they receive. It is only when the nontrained teacher confronts a class of culturally deprived students that his lack of training prevents learning. But many educators are now aware of the problem, and programs designed specially to prepare teachers to deal with this kind of student are being established. In spite of problems, education in the city is showing some signs of improvement, and more improvement will appear within the next decade.

With the better education for the urban poor will come increased political power. More and more of the poor and members of minority groups will be elected to political office, to state legislatures and city commissions. It can even be expected that the election of Negro mayors in such cities as Cleveland, Ohio, Gary, Indiana, and Montclair, New Jersey, is only the beginning of a trend that will make itself felt in other parts of the country. States will establish more institutions of higher learning in their urban centers, and the ghetto dweller will take advantage of his increased educational opportunities to a greater extent than ever before. We can expect to see the lower class groups placing more and more of their members in positions of responsibility and authority. As they continue education in graduate and professional schools, the urban poor will have an increasingly important representation in the professions, particularly in the teaching profession, at all levels from first grade through graduate school.

Many school districts will continue to have financial problems until additional sources of revenue can be found. The property tax is now as high as practicable in many cities, and further increases will be resisted. If fact, very many school-bond elections were defeated during 1967 and 1968. In California, voters were asked to vote on a proposal that would have cut off property tax revenues for schools. The California Teachers Association spent $800,000 to defeat it. In Oregon, a proposal that would have limited property tax to $1\frac{1}{2}$ percent of value was defeated. But some districts in the West, particularly Seattle, suffer seriously because of the refusal of voters to approve additional school levies. The only answer is more state aid in addition to the federal aid mentioned earlier.

The threat of a teachers' strike will be used to persuade voters to provide additional funds, in spite of laws prohibiting such strikes. There were many strikes of teachers in cities other than New York during 1968, and more can be expected even in states where strikes are so far unknown. While the American Federation of Teachers and the National Education Association will continue to quarrel over the terms "sanction" and "strike," many educational leaders now recognize that there is little difference between the two. As of June 1, 1968, only seventeen of our fifty states had some legal procedures for negotiating issues between teachers and boards of education. But almost all states have laws prohibiting strikes by public employees, including teachers. However, the penalties provided are often so severe that public officials fear to impose them. Strikes by teachers will probably continue until more states pass laws providing for negotiations with teachers.

As the legislatures of the states are reapportioned under the "one man, one vote" doctrine laid down by the Supreme Court, we can expect to see more state help for cities in a variety of areas. But federal aid to cities will continue to be important. As the suburbs grow, the problem of commuting to the city will intensify. It can be expected that more freeways will be built, with federal assistance, in spite of the fact that the building of freeways is, in a sense, self-defeating. But there is now a chance that the federal and state governments may assist cities in the development of excellent mass transit systems, both within the city and from the suburbs to the city. Within a few years it must be recognized that the inner city will not hold any more automobiles, but, with few exceptions, most of the medium-sized cities in the United States have very poor systems of public transit.

The federal government will continue its programs of aid to education in urban areas and will assist the establishment of more urban university campuses. Although the Blaine Amendment, which would have allowed state assistance to parochial schools and colleges in New York, was recently defeated, it may be expected that agencies of government will continue to find ways to assist parochial and other private schools, just as they have in the past.

There will be more laws, both state and federal, designed to protect the consumer, particularly the poor consumer. Some such laws, mentioned earlier, have already been passed. While there is much argumentation over their effectiveness, the precedent has been established, and it may be expected that there will be more and better laws and those that exist will be better enforced than formerly.

It can also be expected that there will be more and better federal legislation designed to assist and protect the elderly of the urban community. Social security benefits are certain to be expanded again, as they have been in the past. Also, agencies of government will doubtless establish additional programs to benefit the senior citizens of the city. The urban universities, with governmental support, will aid some of these programs.

The future of the cities is not so bright as all this would indicate. Ruralism is still a powerful force in state and federal government. The large vote compiled by George Wallace in the 1968 Presidential election even in the large cities of the North is a clear sign of dissatisfaction with present conditions. Many of our leaders have openly stated that the United States is facing a serious crisis in urban affairs. There is great disillusionment with schools and with government on the part of people of all social classes and of all political persuasions. Any leader, whatever his past record, who promises quick and easy solutions to so many problems may expect a considerable following. To many, even the promise that the status quo will be maintained by armed force has some appeal. Wallace's party is continuing its organizational activity and will surely be on the scene again in 1972. There is always the danger that an extremist may rise to power in times of turmoil and unrest.

Some writers have drawn a parallel between the United States of today and the France of the eighteenth or the Russia of the nineteenth century. These writers contend that revolution, similar to the French or the Russian revolution in bloodiness and horror, is now possible in the United States. They see our present situation as so hopeless that they quote William Shakespeare's "So foul a sky clears not without a storm."

On the other hand, our leaders, unlike those of eighteenth-century France or nineteenth-century Russia, seem to be aware of the problems of the poor. No country in the history of the world has ever devoted so much thought and energy to the plight of poor and deprived groups in its society. The poor of our country have been able to rise to positions of power and influence, and they can now get a fair hearing in many cities. If the middle class can be made to understand the seriousness of the problems faced by the urban ghetto dwellers and then bring the power of its influence to bear, we may expect peaceful change at a rate rapid enough to satisfy our depressed minorities.

Many other countries have similar problems to an even greater extent. The misery of the poor in all the countries of Latin America is well known. The lower classes of Spain, Portugal, and Italy live only at a subsistence level. Even in such enlightened countries as France and England, well-defined economic and educational classes exist and upward mobility is not particularly easy. As John F. Kennedy so often pointed out, the United States now has the opportunity, more than ever before, to demonstrate to the world the possibility of peaceful change.

NOTES

[1]Harry N. Rivlin, "A New Pattern for Urban Teacher Education," *Journal of Teacher Education*, XVII (Summer, 1966), 184.
[2]James Ridgeway, *The Closed Corporation* (New York: Random House, 1968).

Index

Index

V

Vairo, Philip D., 41, 52, 85
Van Doren, Mark, 76
Vansburg, 60
Vertical stratification, 15–16
Vienna, University of, 68

W

Wagner, Emile, 94
Wallace, George, 134
Warner, W. Lloyd, 59
Washington, D. C., 60
Washington, University of, 68
WASP, 2, 5
Weber, George H., 88
Webster College, 131
Whyte, William H., Jr., 15
William and Mary, College of, 78
Wichita State University, 48, 69, 122
Wisconsin at Milwaukee, University of, 69
World War II, 7
Wright, Frank Lloyd, 17

Y

Yankee City, 60